"To the world you may be one person; but to one person you are the world."
– Dr Seuss.

Contents

Poetry

iStock.

From The Manse Window

Nature's Calendar

Illustrations by Jim Dewar and Mandy Dixon.

Colours Of The Seasons

GREEN is the colour of spring,
New growth is everywhere,
When birds in chorus sing
Renewal pervades the air!

Blue is the colour of summer
With azure skies so clear,
Joy for every beachcomber
When sapphire skies appear.

Gold is the colour of autumn,
Rich shades on all the trees,
Just months ago fair blossom
Is now sweet fruit to please.

Purple is the colour of winter,
For a royal babe was born,
Gold, frankincense and myrrh –
His gifts on a Christmas dawn.

There are colours for every season
When a rainbow fills the sky,
As Nature gives us due reason
To praise our God on high!

– George Hughes.

Wedding Warning

I **QUITE** like a big wedding and all it entails,
And I love it when good, sunny weather prevails,
Though I have to admit that it does seem quite strange
That folk still take them on with so much to arrange.

There's the disco to book for the party at night
And the headache of getting the timings all right.
It's the bride and her parents who plan everything
As the groom is too busy – he's buying the ring!

They choose bridesmaids as slowly as time will allow;
If they miss someone out then there will be a row!
There's the catering firm and, of course, there's the cake,
And there's no knowing how long that's likely to take.

The reception and venue can't be overlooked
But they must get in soon or they'll be fully booked.
Their relations and friends take some thinking about
Or they'll always regret having left someone out.

The big day is approaching and schedules are tight
But they've still got the taxis and hymns to get right.
They must order the flowers – it's not wise to wait,
Then they hope against hope that they won't arrive late.

But if you have agreed to be husband and wife,
And you're planning to have that big day in your life,
Just remember, when spending colossal amounts
That the wedding's not all – it's the marriage that counts!

– Dennis W. Turner.

Late Snowfall

STEEP, steep into the valley
We descend
To where a charred skeleton of cottage cowers,
Fleshed now with snow.

Then climbing again,
Echoes of our breaths
Piling in drifts against the hill
As we trudge along with wind-slitted eyes.

Muddy ghosts haunt the path,
Their bootprints the limit of our vision,
Yet larks flake from April sky,
Or swirl on high in a blizzard of song.

Snowstorm passes like memory;
Rainbows melt in every tussock,
Dribbling colour like cries of moorland birds
Over an ever-widening horizon.

– Rowena M. Love.

My Secret Place

I'VE found a very special place
Of quiet pools and willow trees;
Swans that glide with ease and grace,
Damselflies and honeybees.

I follow trackways here and there,
Then rest upon a makeshift seat
And find a peace beyond compare
With wildflowers round my feet.

A raft of water lilies lies
Just where a moorhen tries to break
The mirror that reflects the skies,
With ripples training in its wake.

A nimble swallow swoops and skims;
A swan discreetly preens its breast.
Close by the bank a mallard swims
And in the hedgerows blackbirds nest.

Two butterflies dance in the air
Then drift and flutter out of sight.
A brace of rabbits come and share
The tasty grasses to my right.

This precious place will always be
A spot where troubles disappear.
I've found peace and tranquillity;
A secret haven hidden here.

– Dennis W. Turner.

Magic Moments

THERE'S a memory in each moment, in just everywhere I look,
In my ornaments and trinkets, in a flower, a toy, a book.
There's a memory in this tablecloth, handmade by a dear friend;
In my diaries there are pages where my memories never end.

A setting sun, a rainbow, walks and outings by the sea;
As children gathering bluebells, memories flood back to me.
In the sunshine I am dreaming, noisy gulls call as they fly,
I remember childhood holidays – how fast has time flown by!

Sad times softened and cushioned, as the years have come and gone,
This perfumed springtime moment is a gentle, peaceful one.
Underneath my sun umbrella, in the garden, drinking tea,
I smile, for I'm creating yet another memory.

– Chrissy Greenslade.

from the Manse Window

Sea Glass, Jewels From The Ocean

I **WAS** on welcome duty at church one Sunday when a young friend came in with her mummy and daddy. She was carrying a little purse.

"What do you have in there, I wonder," I enquired. "Perhaps some pennies?"

She shook her head shyly.

"No."

"Perhaps some crayons, then?"

Again another shake of the head.

"It can't be a teddy!"

She laughed.

"It's my sea-glass collection."

She opened her purse and out on to her hand she poured its contents, precious little pieces of sea glass which would have been painstakingly searched for along the nearby beaches.

Each one in this lovely collection of rounded pieces of green glass had been sculpted by the sea over many years. The glass had been dashed and splintered and tumbled and rolled about in the waves and currents, as though in a giant washing machine, for perhaps as long as 20 or 30 years.

As an eager shell collector myself, I was thrilled at the joy this hobby was bringing to my little friend.

How is sea glass formed? At some time bottles and jars have ended up in the sea, perhaps carelessly thrown from a boat, or left on the sand after a picnic. The waves and the tides have then tumbled these broken shards over and over again, day after day, wave after wave, until all of their edges have been smoothed and rounded off.

At the same time, the seawater has reacted chemically with the glass, pitting and frosting its surface. The relentless action of the sea has transformed these broken, discarded glass bottles into colourful gems which are eventually cast up on to the tideline amid seashells and seaweeds.

The colour of sea glass depends on its origin. The most common colours are green, brown and white, the green and brown from bottles of wine or beer, and the white, clear ones from glasses or jars or window-panes. Less common colours range from jade to amber to purples.

You might even be lucky and find a piece of deep blue sea glass. Could this one perhaps have come from an old Milk of Magnesia

iStock.

By Janice Ross.

bottle? Antique black sea glass is the rarest find.

Before the mid-1960s everything came in glass bottles or jars or tin cans. Now, of course, we have plastic. As a result of this new packaging, these lovely beach collectibles are vanishing. Recycling has also reduced bottle finds, but pieces of sea glass can still be found on shores all over the world.

These sea glass pieces reminded me of God's ability to transform our lives. In the beginning God's intention for man was to be made in his image and likeness and to display his glory. Sadly, because of Adam and Eve's disobedience, that image was marred and from sin came brokenness. Like the glass bottles, we may still have some beautiful smooth areas, but we also have sharp and rough edges that need smoothed.

THIS is so easy to observe in young children. A very small child is totally self centred. He can be happily playing with a toy one minute, but what happens when another little one comes and wants to play with that very toy? Usually a quarrel, a tussle and tears!

Mothers have to teach children how to share and get along with others. Even at that young age there are rough edges to be smoothed.

When we allow Jesus, the Saviour, to be our friend, then he accepts the broken pieces of our lives and begins to work in us, transforming our sinful natures, planing our rough edges, wearing away our self-centredness. Just as I am sure the glass does not enjoy the continual buffeting of the waves, nor do we always appreciate the situations and circumstances that come our way to change us. And yet it is this constant pressure which transforms us into his likeness.

Paul E. Billheimer in his book "Don't Waste Your Sorrows" offers an answer to the question, "Why are Christians not always spared suffering?"

He answers with the Bible's promise in Romans 8 v28, that in all the things that come our way God works for the good of those who love him, who have been called according to his purpose. God is working out his purposes even in hard times. It is God's desire and plan to conform us to the likeness of his son.

God is committed to us. We can be confident of that.

"He who began a good work in you will carry it on to completion until the day of Christ Jesus." Philippians 1 v6.

God is faithful to what we have put into his hands. He is in the process of making us beautiful in his sight. We are a work in progress.

Like the sea glass, rolling and tumbling in the sea for decades, so God patiently works on the transformation of our lives.

Consider for a few moments the people you may know who radiate peace or gentleness or a quiet spirit, those you admire and are glad to have as friends. It would be true to say that none of them was born that way. In fact, if you knew the whole story of their lives you would probably discover that they had

experienced trials, difficulties and suffering, from within and without. These are the very things which have changed them.

An old friend passed on this advice to me as a young Christian.

"If you want to make a good and helpful friend, find one that has been through hardship and suffering but still loves and trusts God."

To return to our beautiful sea glass . . .

Because of the strong tidal currents around our shores, and, of course, our frequent westerly gales, the beaches of Scotland can produce many washed-up pieces of sea glass. Apparently the best times to look are during the spring tides and during low tide after a big storm. So good hunting, everyone! If you don't find any, you can be sure young Ailsa will. ■

iStock.

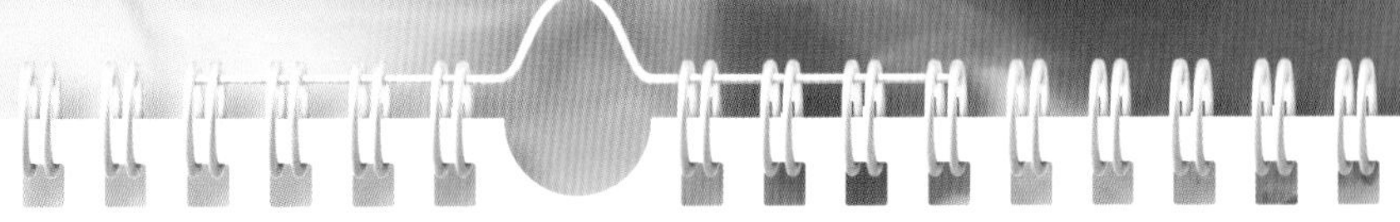

Nature's Calendar For Spring

"Spring" tides aren't just limited to spring – their name refers instead to "springing forth", as it marks the biggest difference between low and high tides, thanks to the alignment of the sun, moon and earth. This happens roughly twice a month.

Queen bees that have survived the winter now begin to appear on flowers, feeding up for the start of their summer season. Should a queen bee die, the worker bees immediately begin feeding larvae of the right age range and start grooming them to take over.

iStock.

In early spring, cold nights but warmer days cause the sap to rise in certain trees as they begin to warm up. The starch stored in the trees converts to sucrose and expands; the pressure then causes it to rise, and – when the tree is cut – run out. This is how maple syrup is drawn.

Lasthenia californica blooms in California early in spring. The flower is known by the name of California goldfields, which perfectly describes the look of them carpeting the semi-arid meadows that they call home.

The acanthus can prove a little unpredictable in flowering – it might even miss a year – but when this Mediterranean plant takes hold, it's worth the effort.

"That is one good thing about this world . . . there are always sure to be more springs."

– L.M. Montgomery.

Light

SOMETIMES it's not about delays and cancellations;
The door that needs repaired, the shopping left behind.
You come home early and find yourself alone:
The sun blooms pink against the kitchen window,
And there's the whisper of a butterfly against the glass.

You slip inside a place where hurry doesn't happen,
And stand there, listening,
As raindrops glisten all the way along the sill.

You scrape a chair back, sit down softly
As though you were in church, your hand across the table.
For in your mind you're back in childhood –
The film of it is faded in your eyes and yet it's there.

And everything you have to do and have to be
Seems suddenly to matter less than what the robin sings
This April evening, as the sun comes glinting here and there
About the house. For all these little things
Are fragments of the light that make up life.

– Kenneth Steven.

Our Camper Van

WE love our little camper van
And use it any time we can.
We tootle round the countryside
And throw the side door open wide
To let in lovely country air;
The sweetest thing, beyond compare.

Our van's quite good enough for us;
It's self-contained; no need for fuss.
It may be small – just room for two –
But there's a sink, a fridge, a loo,
A shower and a cosy bed
That can be used as seats instead.

The cooker's only very small,
But doesn't bother us at all;
It's big enough for us to do
A gourmet dinner, just for two.
We'll take a little country walk
And fill the time with idle talk.

We'll find a spot beside a tree
And have our little picnic tea.
We pack our things and leave the scene
And leave no trace that we have been.
Then very soon we're on our way,
But we'll be back another day.

– *Dennis W. Turner.*

My Collection

I DON'T collect matchboxes,
I don't collect stamps,
I don't collect china
Or Tiffany lamps.

I don't collect statues
With spectacular looks:
My weakness is simple –
I just collect books.

A second-hand bookshop
Is hard to pass by.
"Come in here and buy us!"
The books seem to cry.

"We're old, we've been loved,
But now we're thrown out.
Don't let us be pulped!"
Is their desperate shout.

And not just pre-owned ones.
It's new ones as well:
The feel and the weight,
The look and the smell.

My husband's resigned
To my passion for books.
He doesn't complain:
Just throws martyred looks.

But later this year,
I'm off down to Hay.
I'll come back with more books –
Oh, what will he say?

– Elizabeth Horrocks.

Age-old Complaint

TODAY I'm feeling ancient, though I woke up feeling fine.
No, it's not another wrinkle . . . er, I mean laughter line.
No more grey hairs than yesterday, no more little aches,
No more senior moments or embarrassing mistakes!

No, it's my nephew, Thomas. Now, I adore that boy,
Though he can be exhausting, his visits are a joy
But today, well, it's a pity, I know, and it's a shame,
But facts are facts and truth is, well, Thomas is to blame!

I know it sounds conceited, but it gave me a warm glow
To hear, "Auntie Deb can fix it! She always can, I know!"
If his Action Man was broken or his shoelaces untied,
It was "Auntie Deb, please fix it!" And it cannot be denied,

If he'd torn his brand-new shirt, or tripped and grazed his knees,
I never let him down when he asked me, "Fix it, please!"
I nursed his hamster back to health and taught him how to swim.
Oh, yes, he knew I'd do my best to put things right for him.

But today, well, my computer was truly on the blink.
I simply couldn't fix it, and I'd begun to think
It would cost me a fortune. I let out a woeful sigh,
And then a little figure caught the corner of my eye.

I wailed, "Tom, I've lost my e-mails! I can't get on the web!"
He smiled, then gave my arm a pat. "I'll fix it, Auntie Deb!"

– Deborah Mercer.

Milestones

FOLLOWING my voice,
Newly born, her beautiful eyes found my face.
And love filled my heart.

Clutching bluebells
Newly gathered, her first steps found my arms.
And pride filled my heart.

School uniform pristine,
Newly dressed, her tinkling laughter found my tears.
And fear filled my heart.

Exams now a memory,
Newly qualified, her brilliant results found my smiles.
And joy filled my heart.

Nervous, the boyfriend,
Newly announced, her silent pleading found my approval.
And understanding filled my heart.

Important, the job
Newly acquired, her first-day doubts found my support.
And admiration filled my heart.

With her husband,
Newly married, her radiant beauty found my soul.
And pleasure filled my heart.

Following my voice,
Newly born, her beautiful eyes found my face.
And my granddaughter filled my heart.

– Maureen Walker.

Planting Your Garden

PLANT your garden for today,
Tomorrow is too far away;
The ground might seem uncertain then,
If waiting simply questions "When?"
And know that little can go far,
As light can trace a distant star;
Too much sun can burn, we know,
As tender plants will wilt and show;
So decorate and fill the hours,
Don't wait for someone else's flowers.

And planting leads to deeper thought –
Lessons learned, once known and taught:
A contract lies not in a kiss,
Nor presents – promises like this;
Love does not mean just "leaning" on,
To take and use, depend upon.
And holding hands – it may look smart –
Is far from stealing someone's heart.

So what you sow, make good your store,
And the way you work will thus ensure
The plants you grow in deep, good earth,
Will always prove your true heart's worth.

– Dawn Lawrence.

A Different Kind Of Light

To climb out of the known
Into the moorland's empty miles;
Where sun and shadow meet
And the only elements the ones
That first began this world:
Wind and water, rock and light.

You crouch beside the loch,
Out of the bullying of the breeze –
And nothing might have changed
Since the beginning;
A smear of brightness smiles the water,
Before going back to grey.

Somewhere unseen the sadness of a bird –
A single song in the hugeness of the sky,
And suddenly you know you do not matter
Here beyond the normal and the everyday,
The old enslavement of the hours –
You have escaped to breathe
A different kind of light.

– Kenneth Steven.

from the Manse Window

Come One, Come All

AIRPORTS are fascinating places. As a child it was exciting just to go to Aldergrove in the car to meet visiting relatives and perhaps see a plane take off or land. We have since travelled through some of the world's largest airports with multiple terminals and runways and countless planes. They arrive or depart every few seconds.

I find it a strange mixture of stress and fun, getting the car parked and catching a shuttle bus to the terminal to present ourselves to security (my ever-efficient wife having pre-checked us in online), pay exorbitant prices for coffee then walk miles on those moving walkways to the departure gate before eventually boarding the plane.

Yet it still amazes me a little how someone can be in Donegal, Ireland, for breakfast and in a completely different country speaking another language by lunch or teatime!

Rather like the supermarket checkouts, everything is hi-tech these days. A camera automatically reads my number plate at the car park and raises the barrier. Another device inside scans our boarding cards and grants access. It's the sort of thing that, years ago, would have been classed science fiction, almost like beaming aboard the Starship Enterprise!

iStock.

For me, though, it's the people that make airports so interesting. Huge numbers from every imaginable ethnic background, families, students, professionals, pilgrims, people on holiday, strangers rubbing shoulders. Humans on the move, each with their own unique circumstances, each with their own story. It's the encounters with people I find so rewarding.

Some are unsought, like the lady in dark glasses who grabbed my thigh and exclaimed when our plane hit turbulence.

Or the Italian solicitor with whom we shared a taxi who couldn't understand English people speaking English but could follow our Ulster/Scots dialect perfectly!

Me being me, I usually talk to everyone and am sometimes privileged to share a little of the stories of my fellow travellers. Those who are leaving to explore distant

By the Rev. Andrew Watson.

continents. Those who are coming home for a wedding, or a funeral. Some are relaxed and confident, others anxious and lonely.

The Gospels tell us Jesus looked on the crowds of people and "had compassion on them". These were real people, just like you and me and the folk we meet on our journeys. He knew their stories, their triumphs and joys, their natural concerns, their private doubt, guilt, fear.

He saw it all, and he loved them.

On the cross, Jesus stretched his arms wide to forgive and embrace in welcome those from every nation, tribe and language who trust and follow him. But to him we are not just a crowd of strangers to be noted on computer and managed through "the great airport of life". We are precious individuals, to be befriended, nurtured and loved. One of the amazing, often gradual realisations of Christian faith is discovering that Jesus really knows and loves each one of us personally. What a wonderful discovery it is! How it transforms our worshipping, our praying, our whole outlook on life!

AS we approach another Easter, when we shall reflect again on the wonder of his cross and Resurrection, let's think about a couple of the individuals who encountered Jesus in the Gospels.

The first of these initially seemed like a dream disciple. His story to date had been success all the way. He is described as a young ruler, one "high born" from a respectable and wealthy background. Business was booming and he was riding the wave. Yet he was no playboy, but someone who practised high morals and seemed genuinely interested in spiritual things when he came with his question, "What must I do to inherit eternal life?"

We might imagine the disciples tripping over each other with enthusiasm to welcome him to the group!

However, things took an unexpected turn when Jesus, the ultimate judge of character, discerned that this particular individual had an idolatrous love of money. While the Bible does not teach that having wealth is sinful per se, it was clear the things of God would never have first place in this man's life. So Jesus challenged him to give his assets to the poor if he was serious about following the Christ.

We read a poignant detail, that Jesus looked at this person "and loved him" (Mark 10 v 21). This challenge might seem harsh, but the Lord was being cruel to be kind, knowing the man would be freer and happier without his obsession with possessions. He didn't give his life at Calvary so we could bring our sins with us into his kingdom! We might wonder what he sees as he looks lovingly on us, and what he might want us to change!

And then the disciples looked on aghast as the dream candidate turned and walked away.

"Go after him, Lord! Don't let him get away! Don't be so harsh!"

Jesus's look must have been sad as well as loving, but he let the young man go, and we read he went away sad. There's no record of him ever returning.

By contrast, consider a woman Jesus engaged in conversation by a well in Samaria (John 4).

From a human perspective, everything about this encounter was wrong. She was there in the heat of midday when no-one else was about so she wouldn't have to suffer the critical looks or snide remarks, for her life story had been complex. After a string of broken marriages she must have felt wounded, abused and disinclined to trust people, least of all a man, and a Jewish man at that. She had "baggage", and we can sense the disciples squirming in discomfort as their master reached out to befriend her.

Unafraid, the sinless Son of God looked on this woman as worthy of respect and needful of genuine compassion and love. He offered her a fresh start and "living water". We're not told the detail of how her relationships worked out, but an early tradition gives this lady the name "Photine", meaning "enlightened" or "luminous one", and credits her as someone who became a committed evangelist and martyr for the faith.

Things mightn't have looked that promising at the beginning of their encounter, but how reassuring, how encouraging that Jesus was more than willing to take her on. If Jesus loves and offers grace to individuals like these then there is surely hope for us all, if we're humble enough to receive it!

This Easter, let's look at the crowds, in airports, shopping centres, sports stands, wherever! Let's try to see people as Jesus sees them – imperfect but individually precious, needing love, worth dying for and never beyond hope of renewal and transformation.

Without presuming to guess how the encounter might go, let's seek to introduce individuals to the one who already knows and loves them and gave himself for us all. ■

iStock.

Nature's Calendar For Spring

The buds of the hawthorn burst now in April, with bright green leaves before the white flowers appear. They used to appear in May, but like so many plants these days they're making an earlier start because of warmer winters.

In the US, the mix of warmer air arriving with polar air still descending from the north results in some severe weather. At its most active this time of year is Tornado Alley, a wide area loosely defined as the central states just east of the Rockies.

iStock.

This year, consider planting British wildflower seeds. Mixes are readily available from garden centres, and these native plants are perfect for attracting bees, butterflies, insects and birds.

With the grass now green and lush, cows and deer have plenty to feed on. But did you know that scientists have discovered they both tend to align their bodies in a north-south direction when they eat? Some speculate that it's to do with the earth's magnetic field, which birds also use to navigate.

Malope can be sown directly into the soil around mid-May – or under cover at the beginning of April.

"The point is that the pleasures of spring are available to everybody, and cost nothing."

– George Orwell

Little White Jug

I FOUND a white jug a few inches high,
A strange little jug which I could not pass by;
It serves no great purpose except to pour cream,
Yet so curiously crafted, I stare as in dream.
From the gold-painted rim where the liquid runs out,
There protrudes a wee face which is part of the spout;
A face both mischievous, bearded and bold,
Looking much like a gargoyle from church walls of old.
A swan's neck for handle with beak rises high,
Out from which peers a malevolent eye;
And from where it curves to the end of its base,
There's another small pointed, bold, mischievous face.

Who was it fashioned it, long years ago?
It stirs me to wonder; I'd so love to know.
What impulse empowered the hand and the heart
To construct and contrive such fairy-tale art?
There's a spell I am sure that lurks in it still,
If one looks at it closely that's certain to thrill;
And whoever the potter, I'm sure it was he,
Who once, long ago, had made it for me!

– Dawn Lawrence.

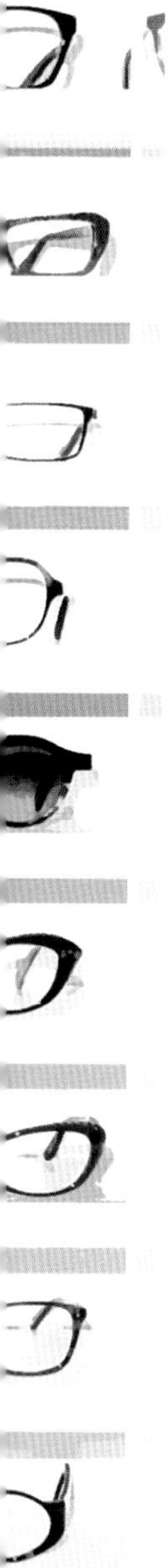

New Glasses

I WAS peering at my laptop –
My eye test must be due,
So I went to the optician's
To see what they could do.

My glasses needed changing –
It came as no surprise.
I decided in that instant
To bring glamour to my eyes!

They showed me to the fitting-room,
Top to floor in frames:
Metal types and plastic,
Some with funny names.

I whittled down to three or four
But then became quite stuck,
And hovered indecisively.
The assistant wished me luck!

I rejected some black sparkly ones,
The brown with leopard spots;
The square frames made my face look odd;
My stomach was in knots.

The assistant, now time challenged,
Was gushing over green
When I spotted in the corner
The loveliest pair I'd seen . . .

They were a jaunty purple
And on them I was sold,
So I left with brand-new glasses
Exactly like the old!

– Marian Cleworth.

Chasing Rainbows

A **SHOWER** of rain and the sun in the sky
Paint a wondrous image that money can't buy.
In the arc of a rainbow the colours shine brightly
And if I could catch one, I'd hold it so tightly.

I'd keep it for ever and not let it go
And whenever I wished, have my own private show.
A riot of colour; a joy to behold;
A brilliant vision more precious than gold.

I saw such a rainbow when I was quite young;
In a bid to get closer I hurried along.
I could see where it ended, just down by the stream.
I ran through the meadow but, as in a dream,

It began to move silently further away
And then, to my horror, began to decay.
Then that wonderful mirage, that source of delight
Became fainter and weaker and faded from sight.

Now, whenever I witness a rainbow display,
I never rush closer and scare it away;
I stop in my tracks and just stand there and stare
And take in its beauty as long as it's there.

– Dennis W. Turner.

A "Budding" Poet

A **ROSE** by any other name . . ."
So said the Bard, but all the same
I still think flowers' names can tell
Us of their essence very well!

Speak of tulips or daffodils
And suddenly the whole air fills
With a sound that seems to sing
Of the promises of spring.

And violet or celandine
Evoke a fragrance dainty, fine,
Modest, shy. But even so,
Determined they will bloom and grow.

Lilac and lavender are meant
To summon up a heady scent,
Colours vibrant, glowing, deep,
And yet a hint of rest and sleep.

Orchid and lily, in this case,
A hint of elegance and grace,
A trifle haughty, words that say
"You do not meet us every day!"

Aster and chrysanthemum
Remind us autumn days will come.
But they are words to bring us cheer
And colour in the waning year.

And then lupin and marigold,
In their very names they hold
A cottage garden, planted, planned,
And tended by a loving hand.

– Deborah Mercer.

Tulip
Daffodil
Rose
Lavender

A Summer Outing

WE'RE off for a day at the seaside!
How's the weather? You never can tell.
The forecast's for sun, but we'd best take our coats
And perhaps some warm jumpers as well.

The grandchildren squeal with excitement
As we pile ourselves into the car.
But soon we hear, "Please, when is lunch? Are we there?"
And we've not even gone very far!

At the beach, we all slap on the sun cream,
Ensuring we won't start to sizzle.
We skip to the sea in our costumes – oh, no!
Big black clouds! And it's starting to drizzle!

We pack up and dash to a café.
"Just a shower," we all – wrongly – agree.
Still, there's something nice about watching a storm
From indoors, with a hot cup of tea.

We venture outside, optimistic.
Should we leave? It's so chilly and grey.
But no, we should all make the most of our trip
And besides, we have come all this way!

So we visit the shops and museums;
All the penny arcades are good fun . . .
Hooray! As we buy an ice-cream on the prom
We're rewarded – with glorious sun!

– Emma Canning.

The Balance Of Nature

IT'S time for picking blackberries
And I know where the best spot is;
A little further down the lane.
Oh, good, I've found the place again.

I've brought a box that held ice-cream
But, whoops! I've dropped it in the stream.
I watch it as it floats away,
But I won't let that spoil my day.

So never mind, my hat will do;
I think it should hold quite a few.
A broken twig has caught my ring;
I'll ease it – drat! I've lost the thing!

I've stripped the branches nearly bare
But all the best are over there.
I lean too far and hear a snap.
Oh, no! There goes my wristwatch strap!

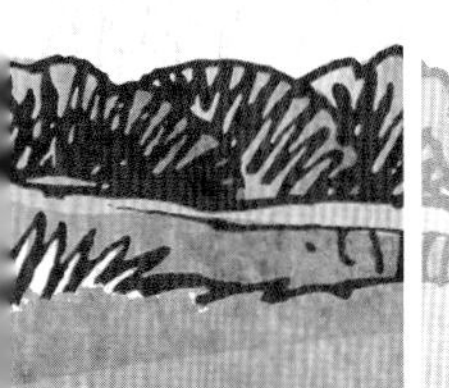

My sleeves are snagged, my trousers torn
And fabric hangs from every thorn.
My shoe is sucked down in the mud
As thorns remove more skin and blood.

I reach out, as it seems OK
To move a branch that bars my way.
The branch recoils back to its place
And whips the glasses from my face.

Well, that's it, then! I can't go on;
My glasses and my watch have gone.
I extricate myself with care
As brambles pull out tufts of hair.

I trudge off home across the field
And nature's balance is revealed:
How many berries I can find –
How many things I leave behind!

– Dennis W. Turner.

The Storming Of Cannich Caravan Park

MARAUDING winds berate the day,
A dark sky claps electric hands.
And rain, attacking, slants its way
Between the tents and caravans.

The trees are on the back foot now;
From raining blows continuing.
Like carousels they buck and bow
And circle in an endless ring.

The whistlers trill, the drummers play
A parradiddle on the tin.
A howling choir leads the fray
In orchestrated battle din.

The park is won, the storm prevails,
The campers fade in sad retreat
And cower 'neath their flapping sails
To contemplate the day's defeat.

– Alan Cornell.

Dressed To Thrill

COWAL is clad in sunshine,
A patchwork of colour and texture
Designed to please the eye.
Beneath her voluptuous curves
A moiré silk trim shimmers with sequins
Among appliquéd craft of every kind.

Yachts tack on the lightest breeze
Like ladies twirling before a fitting-room mirror;
Their reflections wiggle and shimmy
As if trying to squeeze themselves into a boat
That's one size too small.

Heavy rope stitches the ultimate label
To Tighnabruaich pier: the *Waverley*.
Her trademark colours are bright and sharp,
Balanced by the tie-dye version
That bleeds across the water.

– Rowena M. Love.

from the Manse Window

To Be A Child Again

AT the beginning of the summer my friend and I decided to go out for the day. We headed for the Gower coast. It was incredible to think that the last time we did this together was over a decade ago.

Why was it incredible? Because the Gower peninsula is on our doorstep. I live in the Swansea valley, only six miles away from the coast.

When I was a child and a young teenager, my family regularly went to the beach. In those days my parents didn't have a car so it involved at least two bus journeys. Now I have transport I rarely make the trip.

My friend and I had a wonderful day out. The weather was perfect, and because it was early in the season there weren't many people around. We walked on the cliffs at Rhossili before ending up at Port Eynon, where we bought fish and chips and ate them sitting on a bench overlooking the beach.

I re-engaged with all those feelings and experiences from childhood – the smell of brine, the constant shushing of the waves on the sand, the washed-out sunshine sending me to a place of complete relaxation. I recalled building sandcastles, running down sand dunes, eating soggy sandwiches and drinking fizzy pop. I remembered going home at the end of the day with dried sand between my toes and feeling tired from sunshine and swimming in the sea.

It made me think about my relationship with God in two ways – do I take him for granted because he's always there, and have I lost that childhood sense of wonder and exploration?

Many people can't remember a time when God wasn't in their lives. They were christened as babies, sent to Sunday school and then continued to worship.

I was sent to Sunday school, too, but drifted away from church because I knew something was missing. Then, as a student, I had a conversion experience and God became real. I understood what Jesus meant when he said to Nicodemus, "You must be born again."

Nicodemus obviously was a faithful Jew, yet something was missing for him – he'd taken God for

iStock.

By the Rev. Susan Sarapuk.

granted, was content with his level of understanding yet had missed the point of actually having a relationship with God instead of just following a set of religious rules and practices.

This new life in Christ was an incredible experience for me. I felt alive and full of joy. I delighted in prayer and bible study every morning and couldn't wait to get to church on Sunday because I wanted to grow in my understanding.

But that was nearly 40 years ago and there have been times since when prayer, bible study and church attendance have become erratic. At one stage I didn't go to church for two years. I've never doubted the presence of God or my relationship with him; like the Gower coast he's been a place of outstanding (super)natural beauty that is always there, but I haven't always visited.

THE apostle Paul urges us to keep on being filled with the spirit. It's not a "once for all" experience. It's something that continues day after day and we're meant to nurture it. If you've been away from God you can come back at any time and rediscover his beauty. The things you remember will still be there and you'll wonder why you ever stayed away. When I returned to church, God called me into the ordained ministry.

I remember the sense of excitement on the days my family went to the beach. I made plans with my brother.

"We're going to build a car or a house out of sand, we'll play beach tennis and I hope the waves will be big enough to knock us over!"

Sensations were heightened. I recall running out of the sea shivering and being wrapped in a towel and rubbed down, warming up slowly then feeling the heat of the sun on my skin. There was a feeling of safety, contentment and joy, of being in touch with my body and the surroundings.

I wonder how much of that is true as we get older? How in touch are we with feelings and sensations and do we apply this to our relationship with God? I come from the Anglican church tradition where certainly, in the past, emotion in worship has been frowned upon. But can you imagine saying to someone in love that they're not allowed to show it?

When King David brought back the Ark of the Covenant to Jerusalem he danced as he led the procession. We know he sang and played the harp and he wrote many of the psalms. He was a real man, yet he hadn't lost touch with his emotions and he wasn't ashamed to show it when it came to worship. He loved God and wanted to praise him openly.

We can grow cynical and jaded as we get older. We've seen it and done it and the excitement of experiencing new things is past. Yet God is always doing new things and leading us to new places. The problem of many of our churches and us as individuals is that we've grown comfortable with the old things and want to stay where we are. We've forgotten what it is to be childlike and inquisitive. Didn't Jesus say we must become like children to enter the kingdom

iStock.

of heaven? Put away your cynicism. Sometimes it's good to switch off your mind and just feel and experience instead of analysing.

So I will reacquaint myself with what's on my doorstep, and I intend to return to the beach in the summer months. I plan to get into that cold sea and taste the salt, hear the lapping water and gaze up at the blue sky as I backstroke across the bay.

So, too, I must not take God for granted. I need to be open to new experiences and to be childlike as I continue to explore my relationship with him. ■

Nature's Calendar For Summer

If a female zebra finch partners with a less attractive male, she lays bigger eggs. This is in the hope that extra nutrients and space will give the chick a chance to compensate for its poor genes!

British strawberries are coming into season. They were so named in the UK because the berries needed to be protected from the muddy soil through their short season, which was done by spreading straw around their base.

iStock.

Bulgaria's famous Valley of the Roses is in full bloom now. The country is one of the biggest producers of rose oil in the world. The flowers are harvested one by one, largely by women, and collected in willow baskets.

Kupala Night is celebrated in the Ukraine, Belarus, Poland and Russia in early July. The origins of the festival lie in celebrating the importance of water as a bringer of life and nourishment – hence a huge water fight being one of the main events!

Echinops, the globe thistle, looks particularly striking when set amongst other tall plants. It's a magnet for pollinators as well, and will bring bees, butterflies and others into your garden.

"What good is the warmth of summer, without the cold of winter to give it sweetness."

– John Steinbeck

Early Light

THE inky curtain of the dark
Lifts slowly on the day,
As night on velvet-slippered feet
Steals silently away.
And gradually the dawn appears
All flushed with rosy glow,
And sends her golden streamers out
On sleeping earth below.

The silver mist in ghostly gown
Slips quietly out of sight,
A blush of beauty clothes the day,
Bathed in the early light.
Then slowly, as the world wakes up,
There's birdsong in the air;
As little creatures scurry by
There's movement here and there.

A skylark with its fluted notes
Is soaring way up high,
Whilst trees are waving leafy arms
Towards a cloudless sky.
There is a freshness in the air
As breezes dance and play,
And morning splendour blazes in
To welcome the new day.

– Kathleen Gillum.

The Holiday Cottage

IT'S tucked beneath the rolling hills,
Beside the lakeside shores,
A little cottage; nothing grand,
But warm and snug indoors.

It harbours guests throughout the year,
It welcomes every kind –
The young, the old and all who seek
To leave their cares behind.

For here the busy townsfolk head
To find fresh scenes, fresh air,
While others come to walk the hills
Or simply sit and stare.

And honeymooners, now and then,
Who love its gentle peace,
And families who, every year,
Enjoy their summer's lease.

For though so many come and go,
As will so many more,
They know no better refuge than
The cottage by the shore.

– Maggie Ingall.

That August Morning

I REMEMBER a summer
The days hung yellow and wouldn't move,
And I leaned out at night to thick, warm darkness –
The air all made of moths, the trees held breathless.

And when the thunder came I loved the fear of it;
The flickering that lit the hills, the seconds held
Before the grumbling and the boom of anger –
The hissing, singing of the rain.

I remember that morning after storm:
I crept the stairs, went out to stand in sun,
Beneath the shadow play of swifts –
The whole sky blue, the air left deep and clear.

And whether you believe in God or not,
I did that day, still looking up, eyes closed –
My life in purest light.

– Kenneth Steven.

After A Paddle

I **MAY** not be down to the sea again
On our lovely island shore,
Where the water is cold and a deep brown-green
And the breakers crash and roar.

The wind's keen edge, the wavelets' hiss,
Seagull cries and screams,
Wide blue sky and sea-wet stones
All fill my waking dreams.

Among the rocks in sheltered bays
The pools lie small, yet deep;
Unless I stop and sit awhile
Their secrets they will keep.

Braving the wind of the North Sea coast
On a wide deserted strand,
Icy waves turn the feet to stone
Till we run them warm on sand.

I may never be down by the sea again
On a glorious carefree day,
But this I will hold right here in my heart
Though I be so far away.

– Norman Lindsey.

The Winged Artist

I WAKE as a soul enchanted
To a day that is pale and new:
A bird paints a picture before me,
He dips his beak in the dew
And mixes the colours of morning,
Blending them into the blue.

I watch as he draws wide circles
In a flight so rapturous and bold,
Across the shining wake of the sun
Into the clouds' white fold,
And each of his magic brush-strokes
Shimmers in rose and gold.

He weaves the colours of morning
Wherever they gleam and go,
Chasing the netted sunbeams
Like stars in the water's flow
And splashing the rainbow droplets
In the river that runs below.

There's light on the shining feather
That under the swift wing grows,
Like the light that causes a rainbow;
The glow on the mountain snows.
But only the spirit of air can paint
The colours that no man knows.

– Dawn Lawrence.

The Estuary

HIGH summer, and the afternoon seems hardly yet begun,
As hushed and still the riverbank lies drowsing in the sun,
The little boats are moored in lines along the wooden quay,
No urgency to sail away; no other place to be.
A muted creak of movement as the ripples lap the hulls,
A distant flash of whiteness from wings of passing gulls.
A wading bird patrols the bank at slow and stately pace
And sunlight patterns water like a splash of golden lace.
And so it waits, the estuary, till time and tide must creep
And gently wake the river from its soft and sunlit sleep.

– Maggie Ingall.

Sounds Of Summer

THOSE sounds of summer I so love to hear
On long sunny days in the midst of the year:
The buzzing of bees as they're floating around
A rich scented flower-bed, a sweet droning sound.

The cooing of doves from green leafy trees,
So romantic a song, any heart could please;
A peal of bells ringing out from the church
Where a newly-wed couple have sealed their love search.

Clicks of leather on wood from the village green
Where a cricket match makes a traditional scene.
There's a laugh and a splash from the paddling pool
When our dear young children are home from school.

From the seaside big dipper, a screaming screech,
Tinkling harness of donkeys down on the beach.
In the park, a brass band on warm afternoons
Reclining in deckchairs, we hum jolly tunes.

A rumble of thunder on a sultry day
As the heatwave is finally over, they say.
Then tomorrow's dawn chorus will sing out anew
In clearer sweet air, 'neath a sky brightest blue.

– George Hughes.

from the Manse Window

A Link In The Chain

DURING these long summer holidays I tend to hear the same excuse every week, when I go to take a service in different churches. Almost everywhere I go, people are quick to apologise for the fact that there are people missing from their church because they have gone on holiday. I have come to call this "the H factor"!

Contrary to the church stewards' assumptions, I don't begrudge anyone the opportunity to spend a few days away from their usual routine, especially as it is usually well deserved and something they have been waiting for all year. We all need a breather from time to time.

I have a new job (or, at least another job)! Mornings now see me packing my lunch box and going to work on three mornings every week as the circuit administrator. In case people don't know, the word "circuit" is used in Methodism as the name for a group of churches that normally share ministers and many other resources, and help each other out practically and financially.

As a preacher, I have been used to travelling the length and breadth of the circuit on a Sunday in order to help lead worship in some of our churches – some nearer than others. The word "circuit" was first used by John Wesley over 200 years ago, to speak of the area covered by his developing network of itinerant local preachers. Originally, of course, it meant an area that you could travel to on horseback or on foot, as a lot of communities were within easy travelling distance.

Nowadays, though, things have changed. I still rely on horsepower to get me to the church (where my office is based), but it is provided by the local bus company. You are probably asking what this has got to do with holidays. Well, one purpose is to help our new ministers settle in when they begin work in September. So I will not be taking my own "summer" holiday until later in the year.

But that does not mean that I will not take advantage of the summer weather. The office is based in a church with a large glass frontage, so I often take my laptop

By Kathrine Davey, Methodist Preacher.

HAPPY
HOLIDAYS!

computer and forsake the back office to sit in the front of the building, until it gets too hot and I have to scurry back to my cooler back room. In fact, I have commented several times that a good side line for that particular modernised building would be to grow tomatoes, as the front porch often resembles a greenhouse. At these times, I give up my regular companions of the kettle and biscuit tin in search of a cold drink.

A FEW years ago there was no need for a central circuit office, but now the amalgamation of churches into ever-larger circuits and the increasing amount of paperwork involved (where is this paperless society we were promised for the future?) means that it is necessary to have someone to keep the lines of communication open over such a distance.

A little game like Chinese Whispers shows us how the simple task of passing a message on is often fraught with problems. The results of such a game are often hilarious, but it isn't funny if an important message goes astray. I'm sure we all know how easy it is to forget to pass on a message.

The ministers speak of their calling to minister the gospel to God's people, but so often they find this sense of calling is increasingly buried in the bureaucracy that they face in order to do what should be a simple job. So I find my "calling" is to help them to fulfil *their* calling.

In fact, the more I think about it, the more I realise that this exemplifies the church and the wider world in which we live. We need others to help us. Lots of the little jobs that they have to do, like photocopying or printing out a song sheet, can be very time-consuming if it is seen as yet another chore that we don't really have time for, amid all the other day-to-day pressures. Yet those are the kind of jobs that I can easily do at the same time as something else.

By that I mean I must rely on the murmuring of the photocopier in the corner whilst sending out important e-mails. It's a feat that can only be achieved if I have set up the photocopier correctly, which depends upon considerable practice – and my pile of scrap paper will bear witness to the number of times I have failed in this challenge!

This multi-tasking is often rewarded by a few minutes wandering around the building, appreciating the coolness of the sanctuary and reading the many plaques of those dearly loved departed stalwarts of the church who held important offices long before my arrival. I realise in these moments of reflection that I am not indispensable and people have been involved in church work, including running holiday clubs, for many years. In fact, since the foundation of the Church of Christ.

John Henry Newman wrote and meditated on the following words:

"God has created me to do him some definite service, he has committed some work to me which he has not committed to another, I have my mission . . . I am a link in a chain, a bond of connection between persons."

Sometimes I don't feel like a "link", and I am sure that many don't, so I have to keep telling myself that this job was created because of a need and is one which could so easily have remained unfulfilled if no-one wanted to be that link. In summer links are all around us – summertime is the link between the new growth of spring and the autumnal harvest.

We are the link between others, even when we fail to realise it. ■

iStock.

Nature's Calendar For Summer

In Alaska, the salmon are starting to make their run up the rivers to breed. From mid-July to around October, thousands make the journey to the site of their spawning. Although waterfalls and weirs present obstacles, salmon have been recorded jumping nearly four metres to clear them.

Rainbow eucalyptus thrives in tropical forests with wet climates. The incredible bark colour is produced when the bark sheds at different times throughout the year. The inner, bright green bark is revealed, then changes colour through different tones, producing a splattered paint effect.

iStock.

Blackberries are starting to appear in hedgerows around the country. They were used by native Americans to dye animal skins, and the ancient Greeks and Romans used them as medicine. Unsurprising, really, as they're full of flavanoids, Vitamins C and E and manganese.

The Puck Fair in Killorglin, Ireland, is centred around the declaration of a wild goat as the King of the town, or King Puck. In what is a real-life wild goat chase, a catcher will head up into the hills and bring one down into town, where it will reign for three days before being returned to the wild. The goat's welfare is monitored the whole time by an independent vet!

Now that irises are nearing the end of their flowering, it's time to pick the right parts of the plant to keep for next year. Chosen now, a bit of autumn warmth will help settle them in for a good display next May.

"Summer afternoon – summer afternoon; to me those have always been the two most beautiful words in the English language."

– Henry James

Fine And Dandy

To you and me it's a dandelion,
A weed with a goldilocks top,
But to that little elf, all greenly clad,
It's perfect for setting up shop.

And there he will sit, with his legs criss-crossed,
An acorn cap on his head,
With needle and scissors and thimble to hand,
And spools of invisible thread.

Each outfit he makes is "designer", "bespoke",
Fulfilling a special request,
For fairies can't flitter or flutter about
Unless they are looking their best.

His fabrics are moonbeams and starlight and mist
And sunbeams and raindrops and dew,
And all have been wrapped up in rainbows awhile
To give them a magical hue.

There's spangly cobwebs for trimmings and such
And small wisps of cloud from the sky,
And even a pinky white petal or two
Donated by daisies close by.

So next time you're out and you notice
A dandelion, take care,
For there'll be a tiny wee tailoring sprite
Stitching enchantment somewhere.

– Tricia Sturgeon.

Lakeland Cruise

COME with me on a Lakeland cruise,
The day is calm and still,
The sky is blue, the clouds are soft
And touch each distant hill.

We're sailing gently round the lake
As swans go gliding by.
A skylark singing up above
Now lifts our spirits high.

Our shoulders feel the warming sun,
Our hearts feel quiet peace.
This day will make a memory
Which never will decrease.

So come with me a little while
And leave the world behind;
This soothing meditation
Can ease a troubled mind.

And then go forward once again,
Tomorrow must begin.
But store this scene within your soul
To calm you, deep within.

– Iris Hesselden.

Staying Power

THE hours were filled with sunshine.
Cloudless was the sky
When you and I were small and young,
And Time was sweet and shy.
And all the world, oh, all the world
Was ours, both near and far;
Lane and meadow, glade and wood,
And sea and sand and star.

Each dawn brought new horizons
With treasures to be found.
The seasons simply carousels
As Earth went round and round.
Sometimes you'd rescue me from harm,
A shining knight and true.
But then, in turn, to keep things fair
I'd have to rescue you.

The bluebell woods were magical
And fairy-filled, no doubt.
The quarry, though, housed goblins and
A big sign said *Keep Out*.
Tiddlers in a jam jar,
Admired and then set free.
Washes in the kitchen sink,
Bread and jam for tea.

We thought those days of daisy chains
Would never, ever end.
They did, of course, but what of that
When you are still my friend?

– Tricia Sturgeon.

autumn

Starling Flight

AS evening falls, the sun is low,
Suddenly the twilight glow
Is darkened by the swirling crowd
Of starlings in a moving cloud.
Thousands, ten thousand, I see,
But formed into one entity.
One giant bird, they hover, swoop,
Pause a second, swerve, regroup,
Briefly disappear, and then
As quickly they fly back again.
Thousands, ten thousand circling
  round,
Wings beating, yet without a sound,
As if they would defy the night,
A giant ghost in restless flight.

– Deborah Mercer.

Memories

I RECALL those childhood days,
Such a joy to be alive.
Learning all the country ways;
Watching bees around the hive.

Carefree romps down country lanes;
Picking bluebells in the glade;
Threading stems for daisy chains;
Hearing skylarks serenade.

Jumping puddles; getting wet;
Finding easy trees to climb;
Sticklebacks caught in a net;
Losing any sense of time.

Watching spiders catching flies;
Chasing butterflies in flight;
Sounds of raucous pheasants' cries;
Rabbits bounding out of sight.

Knocking conkers from the trees;
Damming streams with twigs and rocks;
Hollow stems for shooting peas;
Blowing dandelion clocks.

All these things and thousands more;
Memories from days gone by;
Precious moments held in store;
Memories that never die.

– Dennis W. Turner.

Her Finest Season

AUTUMN strides in unafraid –
She wears bright colours; she is not staid.
Her deepest reds blow a fulsome kiss
From a mouth which smiles and hides a promise.
Her golds now streaked, still her crowning glory,
Her deep brown eyes mirror life's full story.
Her voice is mellow, rich and warm,
Like autumn's sun it attracts and charms,
She is not shy like the timid spring,
Her colours are strong and full of zing,
Summer's hues both glaring and bold
Now softening into autumn's mould.
She has lived her life with its storms and stills;
She is confident, happy, calm and filled,
Like the autumn fruit, so rich and ripe,
Like those autumn colours so boldly bright,
So, when autumn strides in unafraid,
She smiles, content in the life she's made.

– Thea Morgan.

Autumn Dawn

A **RISING** tide of birdsong breaks
The silence of the night
And, in the east, the faintest gleam
Of early morning light.

No breeze disturbs the stillness of
The chill September air,
And on the ground the dew creates
A carpet everywhere.

The skyline trees make silhouettes
Against the glowing sky
Where streaks of cloud form golden shapes
So pleasing to the eye.

A host of warming colours paints
An ever-changing scene
As reds and yellows flood the realm
Where only black had been.

Then, breasting the horizon, comes
A glimpse of golden sun;
A slow majestic rising as
His reign has just begun.

The crowing of a farmyard cock
Accompanies the dawn.
The rising sun lights up the sky.
Another day is born.

– Dennis W. Turner.

Travelling To Tintwhistle

AUTUMN chemistry makes colours swirl and boil
In the valley's cauldron. Sulphur, bronze and copper
Leaves overflow into the gutter in a haphazard sputter,
Where they'll ripple and roil by the roadside
Until alchemy turns them to lead.

On the climb to the moors,
Above a generous measure of ferrous ferns,
Deer grass fizzes and burns
In every shade of orange and brown,
While in the distance a bonfire steams.

We drive on towards Tintwhistle,
The Longendale Reservoirs glinting mercury
In the growing gloom; sunset over the escarpment
Giving one last splurge of heat
Before the view turns to charcoal and ash.

– Rowena M. Love.

from the Manse Window

An Extra Harvest

JOHN and Diana have spent most of their lives living and working abroad. It's been a rich, fascinating existence for them, and one which – I suggested – must have left them feeling a little flat now that they have retired and are back home for good.

"Not a bit of it!" John grinned. "It's been a real pleasure to be able to start joining local clubs and societies, and get involved with the community. And as we both love gardening, it's also been great to have the chance to take on an allotment and start growing things. And best of all, we like having proper seasons again!"

Seasons. Yes, indeed. For those of us who have not spent years living in hotter climes, it's easy to take for granted the fact that here in Britain the weather and temperature will change throughout the year. Yes, we might grumble about its fickleness (who, me?), but I for one would not really like to wake up knowing that today's weather will be exactly the same as the day before, and the day before that.

I really do like the crisp snap of winter and the sight of graceful leafless branches silhouetted against a clear frosty sky. I like spring and its dancing daffodils and catkins. I like summer, with its lavender and lupins, its showers of roses filling the warm air with their delicious perfume. And now that we are back in autumn again, I am reminded that I particularly like this present season for its – vegetables!

Very well, I'll admit that vegetables may lack the immediate glamour of some of the other garden stars, but it's undoubtedly autumn that provides the best food for the body as well as the eye. Even the fields and hedgerows seem eager to supply us with a feast of free seasonal delights such as mushrooms, damsons and blackberries, while markets, shops, and gardens are overflowing with juicy plums, apples and pears, cauliflowers and kale, peppers and parsnips, fat striped marrows and pumpkins the size of beach-balls. Too many good things not to share!

Perhaps that's why one of my favourite annual events at our church is the Harvest Festival service. Being curious, I once did a little

By Maggie Ingall.

research on the subject and found that some form of celebration of the fruition of the crops appears to have taken place in Britain since pagan days.

The gathering of the new wheat was marked by Lammas Day, the first day of August, and it traditionally involved the making of special loaves of bread. This would either be broken into four pieces and placed in the four corners of the barn to protect the gathered grain or, in later times, taken to church to be used as communion bread.

But the first actual form of harvest festival as we would recognise it today did not happen until the middle of the 19th century – comparatively recently in the long history of harvest time. And it was all brought about by a clergyman by the name of Robert Stephen Hawker.

He was born in Plymouth in 1803, the eldest of nine children, and although he was an able student he was also a troublesome and unruly one, who ran away from more than one school. Perhaps it was just as well that he appears to have been possessed of such a robust personality, for he was going to need it!

Hawker's decision to enter the church as a profession might have seemed a fairly safe and conventional one, but after being ordained in 1813, he was sent to the parish of Morwenstow, where he was to discover that being a vicar in Cornwall was decidedly challenging. These were still lawless times in the West Country, with scant respect for either civil law or religious teachings, and where smugglers and wreckers flourished openly.

A man of conscience and compassion, Hawker was greatly distressed by the shipwrecks that occurred so close to his home. He did his best to cajole or harangue reluctant boatmen into saving as many lives as they could, and also tried to ensure that any drowned seaman was at least given a Christian burial. Using flotsam and timbers from the wrecks, he also built himself a little hut on the cliff-top to be used as both his lookout and his refuge.

Yet as well as fulfilling his duties as a clergyman, Hawker had many other interests. He was an antiquarian, deeply interested in Cornwall's rich and fascinating history. He was a writer of both prose and poetry who, among other works, penned "The Song Of The Western Men" – famous for its lines:

"And shall Trelawny die?

Here's twenty thousand Cornish men will know the reason why!"

Hawker was never going to be a conventional clergyman. Eschewing the usual sombre garb of his calling, he insisted upon always dressing in bright clothes, which often included a yellow poncho and a pink hat. He loved both birds and animals, kept a pig as a pet and is reputed to have excommunicated one of his many cats for chasing mice on a Sunday. A colourful character in every way.

But there can be no doubt that his lasting legacy remains in his introduction of the modern harvest festival.

It was in the autumn of 1843 that Hawker first came up with the idea.

iStock.

Pinning a notice to the door, he invited his parishioners to come to a special Sunday service which would be dedicated to thanking God for the annual bounty. He also invited them to bring whatever garden produce they could spare. The resulting harvest was then distributed to the poor of the parish.

It was an innovation that was quick to spread, first throughout the neighbourhood, and then throughout the country.

Nowadays we take this annual festival for granted, but it is worth remembering those humble beginnings that happened not so very long ago.

Yet despite all the autumn goodies available, I often feel that autumn offers an extra harvest that is not quite so tangible, but which can be shared by everybody – a harvest of nourishment for the soul.

Who could not look upon the vivid colours of the trees without a lift to the heart?

Who could not marvel at the intricacy of a dew-dropped spider's web in the hedge, enjoy the tang of a distant leafy bonfire, relish the smell of a fresh-picked apple, or enjoy the crunch of drifting leaves beneath the foot?

Oh, I really do like the annual change of seasons, and autumn in particular! ■

Nature's Calendar For Autumn

Over the last 40 years, whale songs have been getting progressively deeper. No-one knows why, but a definite difference of a few hertz has been registered during that time.

Lettuce continues to grow well even now. It belongs to the daisy family, and was first cultivated by the ancient Egyptians who initially considered it a weed. More than half the world's lettuce supply now comes from China – over 10 million tonnes.

iStock

The Qiantang River in China has one of the world's largest tidal bores, which often occurs in the autumn. Reaching up to 30 feet high with speeds of 25 miles per hour, it's caused by a surge of incoming tide. Surfers regularly attempt to ride the waves, but they can be a bit choppy!

China's mid-autumn festival is one of the most dazzling events around, with the whole country taking part in displays of light, fireworks and offerings of food. It's often called the moon festival, as it occurs on the night of a full moon. An ancient Chinese poem says, "May we live long and share the beauty of the moon together, even if we are hundreds of miles apart." Vietnam also celebrates the same festival.

Crown alliums, a type of ornamental onion, are a beautiful burst of colour and now is the right time to plant them. Even after the flowers have faded, the seed heads are still charming.

"Autumn is a second spring when every leaf is a flower."
– Albert Camus

The Statue In The Park

SHE stands there in the quiet park,
A dainty figure, quite alone;
She wears a pretty dress with frills
And carries flowers made of stone.

And there she stands, year in, year out,
Hand raised in such a pretty pose,
Her face, serene and calm, smiles on
Through summer sun and winter snows.

Sometimes a passing family
Will say, "Poor thing, she's all alone!"
But they don't need to pity her
Because her heart is made of stone.

– Eileen Hay.

Letting Go

IT only seems like yesterday
I'd rock you to and fro,
And sing a gentle lullaby
Till off to sleep you'd go.
My little tot has now become
A boy of five years old,
Jumping, running, kicking balls
And confidently bold.

For you've outgrown those baby years,
It's time to stretch and grow,
And so it is with smiles and tears
I have to let you go.
A whole new world is opening up
Which will develop you,
You'll learn to read and write and sketch –
There's many things to do.

Suppose you fall and scrape your knee
Or someone pushes you?
I won't be there to hold you close
Or show you what to do.
But here, at last, this day has come.
I'm trying to play it cool,
My heart is torn – I feel forlorn –
It's your first day at school.

– Kathleen Gillum.

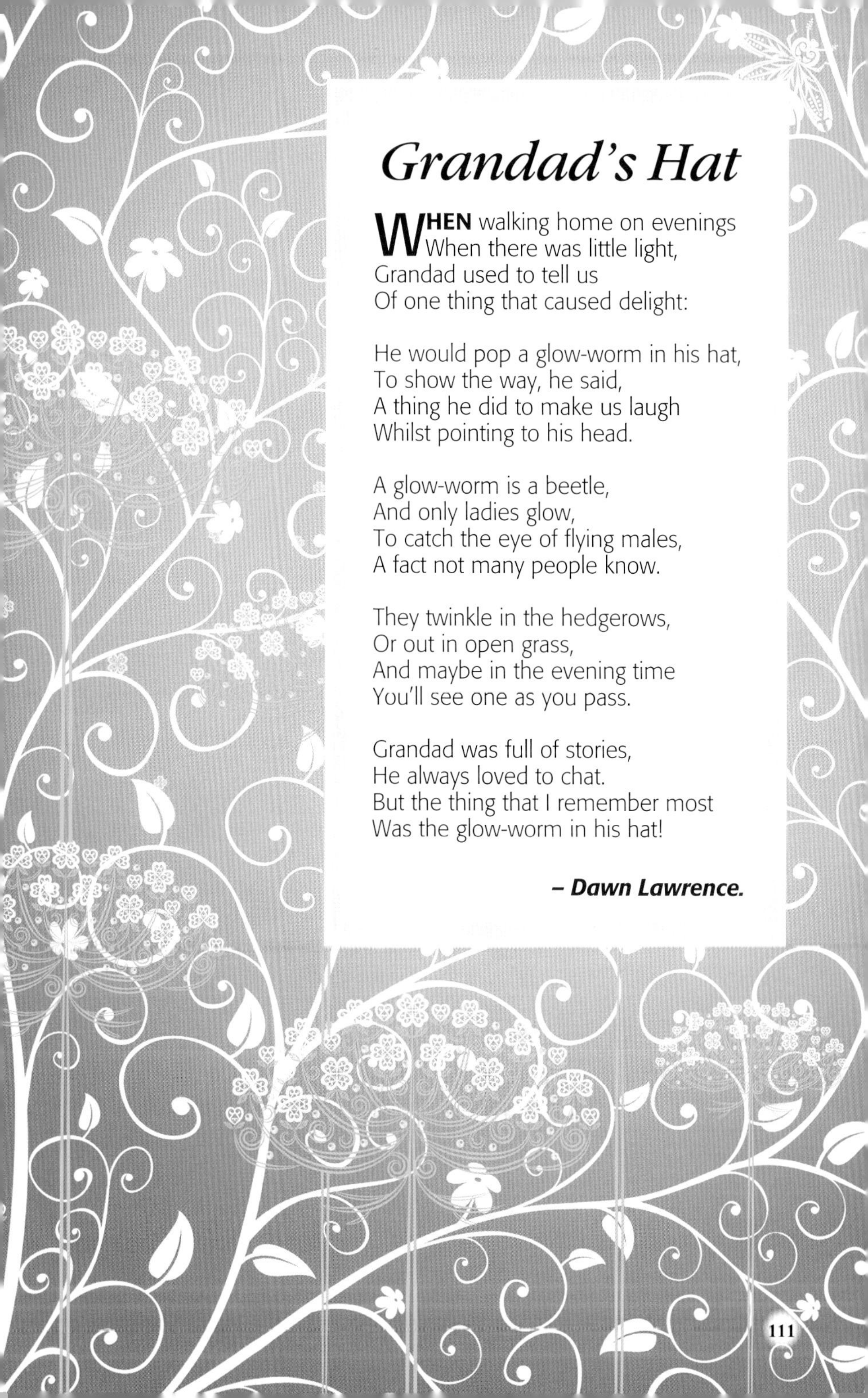

Grandad's Hat

WHEN walking home on evenings
When there was little light,
Grandad used to tell us
Of one thing that caused delight:

He would pop a glow-worm in his hat,
To show the way, he said,
A thing he did to make us laugh
Whilst pointing to his head.

A glow-worm is a beetle,
And only ladies glow,
To catch the eye of flying males,
A fact not many people know.

They twinkle in the hedgerows,
Or out in open grass,
And maybe in the evening time
You'll see one as you pass.

Grandad was full of stories,
He always loved to chat.
But the thing that I remember most
Was the glow-worm in his hat!

– Dawn Lawrence.

A Stately Life

"THE portico is Georgian," our guide was keen to tell,
"Most perfectly proportioned, and beautiful as well.
And here, as now we enter, enjoy the marbled hall,
Where portraits of past lordships look down upon us all.
The statues here are Grecian; they line the graceful stair,
Now come and see the library with books both old and rare.
And here – no, please don't touch, sir – the state room can be found,
It boasts exquisite paintings; fine artifacts abound."
I glanced towards my husband, and he glanced back at me.
"D'you think," he whispered softly, "that the café boasts nice tea?"
We slipped away unnoticed, as quiet as a mouse,
Most grateful that our own home was not a stately house!

– Maggie Ingall.

Wind

ST KILDANS were born into storm:
All winter long a buffeting and tugging,
The hurrying sky above.
They grew up with gale,
Knew the right way
To steer around and against it;
Find a place carved deep beneath it
For light and fire.

When they came to settle on the mainland,
Some in cities, how they must have listened
To the strange silence of the night, hearing
The sweet-soft birdsong in the morning,
Gone out to walk the empty, unheld air
And yearned sometimes for nothing more
Than to climb back inside
Their crows' nest of an island, worried by weather
And held in the wind's hands.

– Kenneth Steven.

Leaning On A Gate

I DON'T stride out or power walk,
But like to stroll and look at things,
To lean upon a five-barred gate
And feel the peace that nature brings.
I wander, saunter, breathe the air –
For someone city-bred like me,
With air this pure and cut-grass fresh,
There's nowhere else I'd rather be.
Each season brings its own reward –
The joy of seeing the first spring lamb,
Then summer cows with swishing tails
Just grazing daisies, lazy, calm.
The seasons turn with autumn leaves
Of reds and golds that seem to glow,
And then, most magical of all,
A winter sun on tranquil snow.
Such sights are nurture for the soul
And so the busy world can wait,
I'm not quite ready to return
As I am leaning . . . on a . . . gate!

– Eileen Hay.

Summiting

STRETCHING out away from me the track is very clear,
The clouds are high and up above the summit looks quite near.
My boots are worn but comfortable; my lunch is in my pack,
I have my map and compass here, in no time I'll be back.
The slope is getting steeper now, the path is narrowing down.
The twists and turns all hurt my knees; my smile turns to a frown.
I stop and drink some water and sit to rest my feet,
My muscles are all aching and a bath will be a treat.
I've nearly reached the top now and can't wait to see the view.
A big deep breath will help me on; I need to see this through.
I can't stand up in all this wind; I'm down on hands and knees.
The forecast didn't tell me this – it said a gentle breeze.
The cloud has dropped, it's raining now – I wish I wasn't here.
If I could just be home again I think I'd raise a cheer!

– Kate Saxon.

from the Manse Window

To Absent Friends

NOVEMBER is the month in which many folk pause to remember. People observe moments of respectful silence and some wear poppies as they think of those killed or injured in the seemingly endless wars around the world.

Memories are something we all have. Some may bring us regret, but others we cherish and love to call to mind. Often, during wedding receptions, people will stand and drink a toast "to absent friends", remembering with gratitude, pride and undying affection those who have enriched our lives but are no longer with us.

Frequently it doesn't take a special occasion. Anything can do it. We discover a card or letter in a drawer, or hear some old song on the radio, and we're away, transported back years, hearing their voices again, basking in the warmth of their smiles.

My dad didn't serve in the Army. He didn't parachute into enemy territory with a machine-gun. He was never awarded medals for bravery. He didn't have that kind of glamorous macho image I used to admire as a child. But as time passed he became, and will always remain, a hero to me.

He wasn't that spectacular. He was just a man who loved my mum faithfully for over 60 years. He worked every day and came home for tea. I realise now how precious that was.

Afterwards he would don his brown shop coat and disappear to the garage for a bit of DIY. He was brilliant at decorating and woodwork, talents I never seemed to inherit despite being often enlisted to help. I didn't mind a break from homework, though, to "hold a piece of wood" while Dad drilled or sawed.

He would come in on time for one or two favourite programmes like "Only When I Laugh" or "The Good Life", when we would all pile on to the settee and split our sides laughing.

Dad was an Elder in our church, where he and Mum both sang in the choir. We went every Sunday, twice. No-one ever thought of going anywhere else. I can remember both my parents kneeling on the floor beside me at bedtime, teaching me as a young child to say my

iStock.

By the Rev. Andrew Watson.

first prayers.

Our family didn't travel beyond the UK in those days, but I remember Dad taking us on holiday in the car on the ferry to Stranraer, Scotland. That seemed a big enough adventure at the time!

Dad never really appreciated pop or guitar music. It was an alien language to him. In truth he quite disapproved of some of the stuff my brother and I listened to, but he and Mum still sacrificed to buy me my heart's desire for my twenty-first birthday – a Stratocaster guitar which I still play! What an encouragement to trust in our Heavenly Father who delights to give "good gifts" to his children!

Besides hymns, I guess Dad was a classical music man. He introduced me to a few well-known pieces on vinyl records. How precious during his last months to take the mp3 player to his room and remind him of Rossini's "William Tell Overture" or the sweet, gentle "Elizabethan Serenade".

Cerebellum ataxia is quite a rare neurological condition that slowly renders a person severely disabled. We saw its early signs in Dad when I was still in my teens. Stiffness, loss of balance, walking sticks, crutches . . . eventually a wheelchair. Long-term prognosis: gradual deterioration. Cure: none.

It was difficult to accept, with all of us coming to terms with it in different ways.

The real inspiration was Dad himself, who trusted God for grace to face whatever would come, and practised an amazing patience and cheerfulness through it all.

I think of him now with such pride, slowly making his way on crutches into the hall to teach his Sunday school class, or getting hand controls in the car so he could still take Mum to the shops. Giving the grandchildren rides in his chair. Charming the staff in the nursing home with his typical friendliness and good humour.

And I'm sorry. Sorry I didn't always appreciate him. Sorry that we didn't go more walks when we could. But I'm also glad because I know he loved me and the last thing I heard him say was my name. And I'm glad we were with him as he passed over to be "with Christ, which is far better"; glad and honoured that we could carry his coffin to the resting place to await the resurrection at our Lord's return.

Dad died in September 2014. And I miss him. I hope he would be happy with how we're all turning out. I think he would be just as encouraging as ever.

Memories such as these are indeed precious. It is good to remember family and friends, dear people who have touched our lives, particularly those who have comforted us with their kindness or inspired us with their example.

The Old Testament book of Proverbs in its closing verses praises a wife and mother of noble character whose adult children publicly "rise and call her blessed" for the example she has given them in hard work, integrity and charity.

iStock.

King David never forgot the friendship once shown him by Prince Jonathan when he was little more than a young shepherd boy. Years later, David sought out Jonathan's last remaining relative, Mephibosheth, and showed him generous kindness for his father's sake. Good memories from the past should prompt us to good actions in the present.

The New Testament writer to the Hebrews by way of godly example calls to mind in Chapter 11 the stories of numerous characters in the history of God's people who learned to "walk by faith". Abraham, Moses, Gideon, Samson, David, Samuel – the list is a long one. He describes them now as a "great crowd of witnesses", almost like a stand full of sports fans, cheering us on as we seek to follow and serve Jesus.

And Christ himself is the one we should remember most often, the one who on the first Good Friday willingly laid down his life that we might be friends of the Son of God. The previous night, at the Last Supper, Jesus instituted the sacrament of Communion, saying, "Do this in remembrance of me." Christians remember and look to him whose cross and resurrection are for us the promise of eternal life.

That's why we don't grieve our loss "as those who have no hope" but as people living in anticipation of resurrection and glory. By his grace I know I'll see Dad again. Still smiling encouragement, no doubt, but no longer disabled. We'll get another chance to take those walks.

I look forward to that . . . ■

Nature's Calendar For Autumn

In late autumn, the north American population of monarch butterflies migrates to Mexico. Not one of the butterflies that starts the journey will finish it, but the females will lay eggs along the way and their children will complete the migration.

Pumpkin, the classic autumnal squash, is often associated with the US and Hallowe'en carving. They've been grown in North America for 5,000 years and are indigenous to the western hemisphere. A French explorer was the first western European to come across them, and called them "gros melons". The name became "pompions" in English, eventually evolving into the word we know today.

Harvest festivals are an age-old tradition, all around the world. Often we think of this as a time of bringing in the last of the year's crops, when all the village would have mucked in to prepare for winter, but many other harvest celebrations happen at this time of year, giving thanks for everything from fish to bread.

Japan's famous for its cherry blossoms, but it also puts on a spectacular autumn display. The Japanese word for the colourful leaves is "koyo", and they have websites charting the progress of the koyo front as it moves its way southwards down the country through the weeks.

Inula in full flower takes up a fair bit of space, capable of growing up to six feet high and spreading nearly three feet across at the lower leaves. It's best planted near short plants or a pond, where its leaves can be appreciated until it comes into flower.

"Autumn carries more gold in its pocket than all the other seasons."

– Jim Bishop

HAPPY BIRTH

The Birthday Card

I **BOUGHT** a birthday card for Nic that cost me seven pounds,
(The kind that, when you open it, makes loud and noisy sounds).
This card was extra noisy, with lots of flashing lights
To startle the unwary and give most people frights.

A New York vista sprang to view, a night-time, lurid scene,
With sky-scrapers that touched the sky and sounds of high-pitched screams.
I thought the card sure to impress despite the crippling cost,
And put it somewhere extra safe in case it should get lost.

But when the special day arrived for the stupendous "splash",
The result was catastrophic! My hoped-for thrill was dashed.
The card was opened, laid aside – I cringed with reddened face,
For not one sound, one flickering light came forth. No, not a trace!

Imagine my embarrassment. No scene can equal that.
The most explosive birthday card had a battery that was FLAT!

– Dawn Lawrence.

A Doggy Dilemma

IT'S said that dogs have owners,
While cats have only staff,
And always, when I hear it,
I give a hollow laugh.

For I, you see, am owner
Of Fritz, my faithful mutt,
So do I have it easy?
You might say yes. Ah, but . . .

Who needs a walk twice daily
No matter if it's wet?
Who needs his dog food fetching,
Or coaxing to the vet?

Who needs an hour's grooming
When steeped in mud and mire?
Yet when I'm wet and weary
It's he who hogs the fire!

So, which is most demanding?
Now, is it mutt or mog?
I only know in my house,
I'm surely not top dog!

– Maggie Ingall.

Smiles

THE visits to dear Aunt Meg
They seem so long ago,
To her cottage in the lovely dales,
The treasures there on show.

A starched and lace-trimmed tablecloth
And vases round the room;
Shelves for all her Toby jugs
And flowers all in bloom.

She loved her aspidistra
And brolly stand, quite rare,
And the antique oval mirror
Taking pride of place right there.

Glasses would be sparkling
When sitting down to dine,
The magic at the table
Her very own potato wine.

To wander through this treasure trove
With everything in place,
Memory still does warm the heart
Of Aunt Meg's room, full of grace.

– Dorothy McGregor.

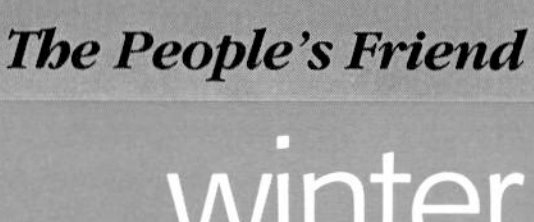

Armistice Morning, Portpatrick

SALTIRE sky waves a flag of freedom,
Sun slashing cold against the blue,
A far cry from the usual weeping rain
As vapour trails fray like memories.
Unfettered hopes drift in cirrus,
Blur to a veil, a shroud
Wrapping the morning in ghosts.

Poppy-coloured trees wreath a graveyard
Full of stones, grey as gunmetal,
Where ancient graves incised with details
Whisper of lives, not death.

A cat, the silver of old souls striped with sorrow,
Watches unblinking while crows stand guard,
Their sentry box just a ruined dovecot.
They caw their challenge to all who would pass,
But the password's long forgotten.

– Rowena M. Love.

The Early Bird

SNOW has fallen while we slept,
Winter-white, flakes fluttered down,
Transformed the lawn, the spell has swept
Away soft green and patchy brown.
Now all is smooth, soft and serene,
A carpet perfect and pristine.

Ivory in morning light,
Beneath a cloudless, ice-blue sky.
But then I smile – a sudden sight
In the corner of my eye
Makes me see my mistake;
I was NOT the first to wake!

A little track, sharp, well-defined,
Standing out upon the snow,
Someone has left his mark behind.
Who could it be? I think I know.
A cheeky robin, morning bright,
Hopped across the pristine white!

– Deborah Mercer.

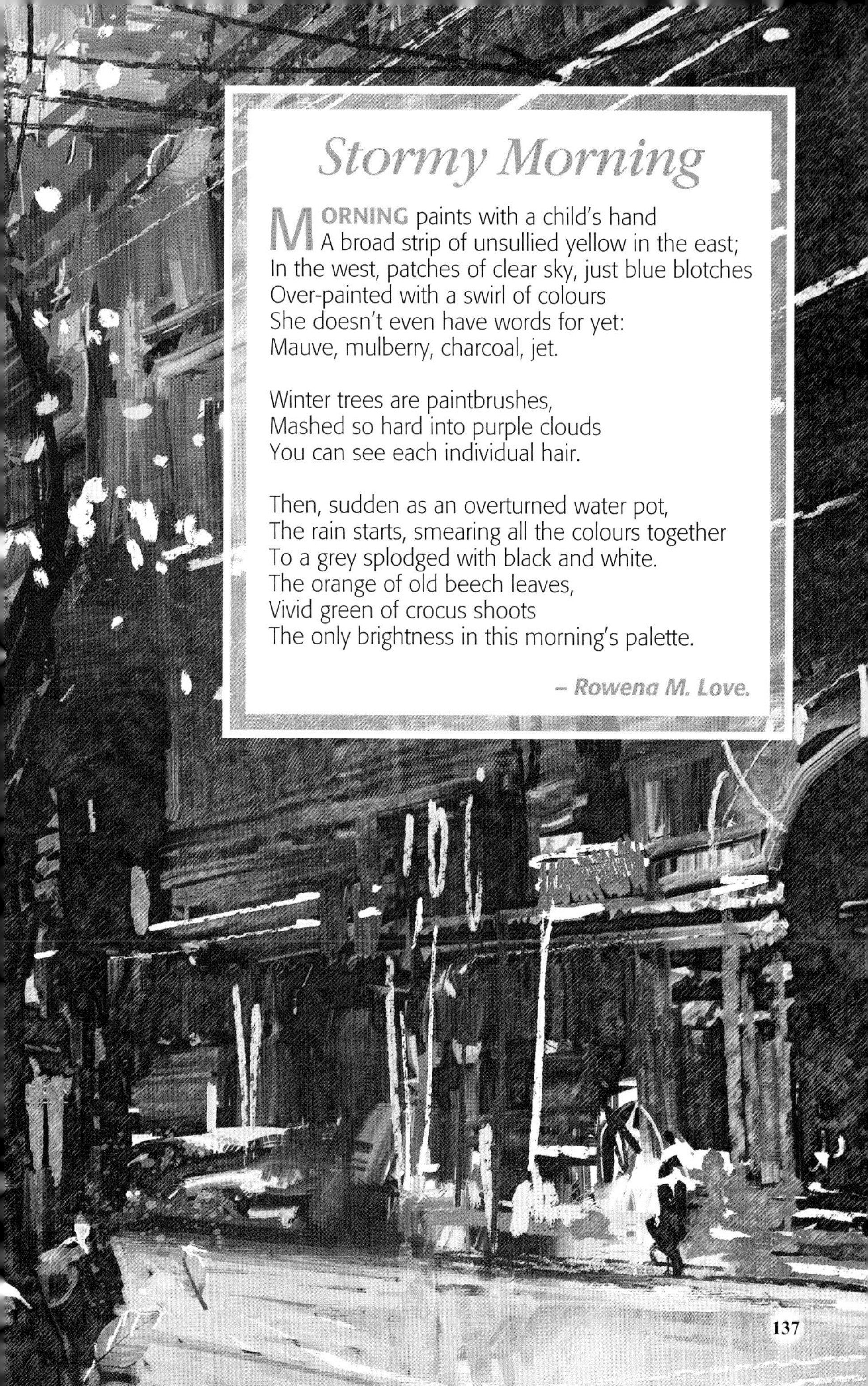

Stormy Morning

MORNING paints with a child's hand
A broad strip of unsullied yellow in the east;
In the west, patches of clear sky, just blue blotches
Over-painted with a swirl of colours
She doesn't even have words for yet:
Mauve, mulberry, charcoal, jet.

Winter trees are paintbrushes,
Mashed so hard into purple clouds
You can see each individual hair.

Then, sudden as an overturned water pot,
The rain starts, smearing all the colours together
To a grey splodged with black and white.
The orange of old beech leaves,
Vivid green of crocus shoots
The only brightness in this morning's palette.

– Rowena M. Love.

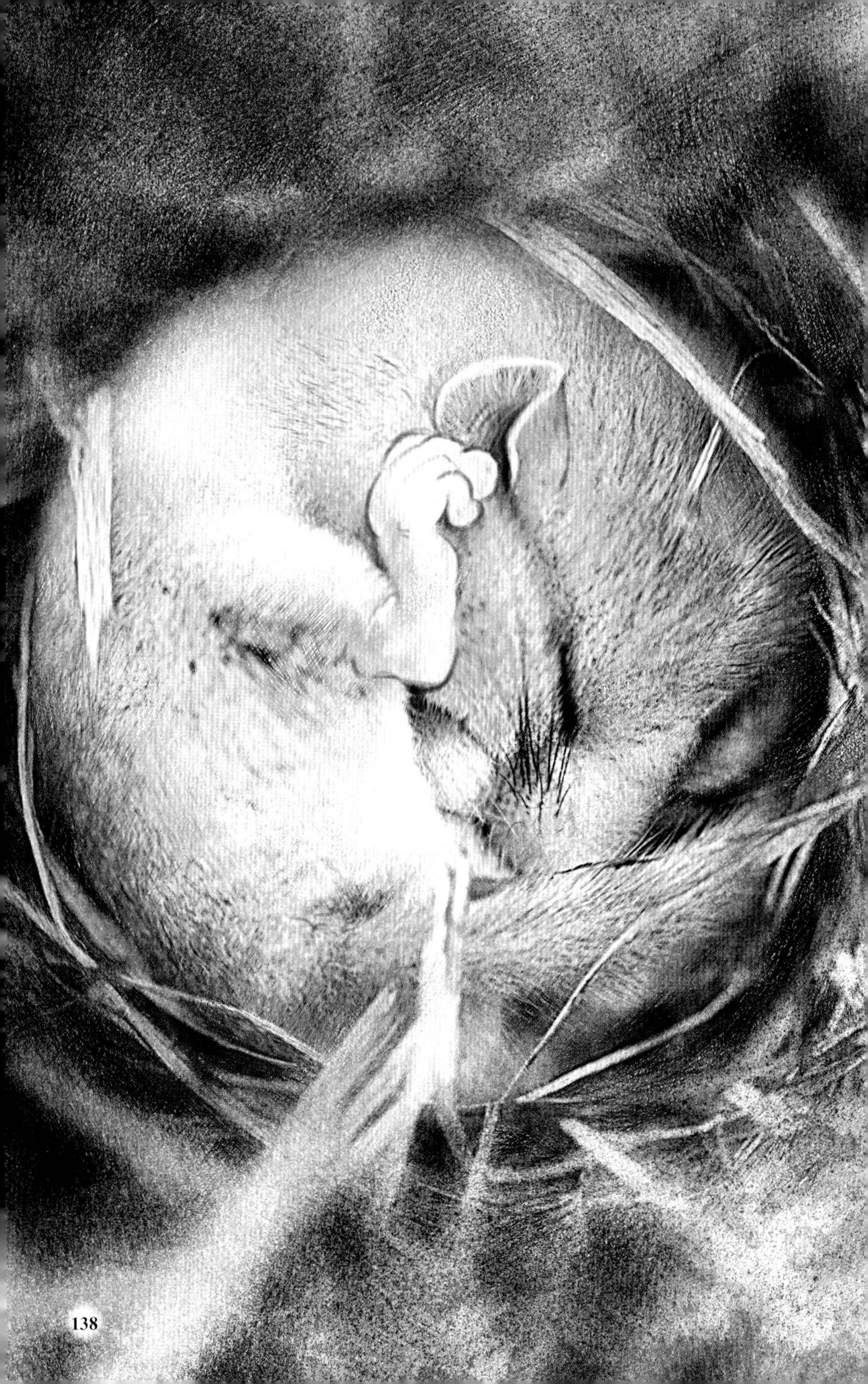

One Who Sleeps

"ELUSIVE" is the word for me –
A creature you may never see;
For in a tree, or on the ground
I'm very rarely ever found.
Dormir – to sleep – should give a clue,
It's something that I'm known to do;
And this, I think, should make it plain
That dormouse is my common name.

My nest, if found, may give surprise.
It's like a tennis ball in size;
And there all day I'll curl up tight:
A tiny ball of gold and white;
By dusk I'm in my active state,
But don't forget – I hibernate!

In summer I will nest in trees,
To feast on nuts I find on these;
In winter, when the cold winds blow,
In hedge or underground I'll go;
And with my tail of fluff – so fine,
No mouse can boast a tail like mine –
I wrap it round my curled-up toes
To hide my head – and warm my
nose!

– Dawn Lawrence.

December School Run

CARS are strung along the road
Like multi-coloured baubles,
Their lights twinkling against
Darkness of pine that lines the way.

Carols belt from the radio,
Ably assisted by the child in the back,
Who has no volume control
Only loud and louder.

Through the village, up the hill,
Where houses are frosted with decorations
That gleam and sparkle
Through the early morning glow.

Day tweaks dawn's dimmer switch,
Turning it bright, bright, brighter,
As prettily patterned clouds fold back
To reveal their gift of blue.

– Rowena M. Love.

from the Manse Window

Give Thanks For Winter

IN his book "The Lion, The Witch And The Wardrobe", C.S. Lewis describes Narnia as a country where it's always winter but never Christmas. I've always considered that to be a wonderfully evocative description, but how depressing.

Winter is a long season made more bearable by Advent and Christmas, with all their accompanying celebrations to lighten the dark days. Then, once New Year is over, it's time to anticipate the spring.

Even though, for me, January is the worst month of the year, it brings hope that dark days will soon be gone and light and life and joy will come again. We can't live without hope and anticipation. A friend says that his birthday always begins the day before and he calls it "Happy Anticipation Day" because looking forward to a birthday is almost as good as the day itself.

Just as the changing seasons are part of life, so it is with changing spiritual seasons, too. Joy and hope come in the morning, dark times pass, winter is swallowed up in the warmth and new life of spring. But there will always be winter, and it's not just a time to get through with your head down; it holds its own beauties and merits.

I love to walk, and one of the things that makes my heart sing in the winter season is the sight of the outline of bare trees. You can see the shapes of the branches, the variety of colour, the light filtering through the tracery of branches, the moss on the trunks, the glistening ivy and tangle of brambles. There is something ethereally beautiful about seeing a tree exposed back to its bare bones.

And the same is true of our spiritual lives. We don't like the dark, dead times but they serve a useful purpose. God is always at work, sometimes even more in the dark times when all the noise and colour is stripped away. It's easy to feel all is well in the height of summer, but when we hit tough times what does our faith say then?

Job is a case in point.

"Oh, sure, your servant is faithful," Satan sneered when the strong faith of Job was pointed out to him. "That's because he's got everything he needs. But take it away from

iStock.

By the Rev. Susan Sarapuk.

him and it'll soon be a different story."

So God permitted Satan to test Job (of course he knew his servant would not fail: He held Job in the palm of his hand). Job proceeded to go through a terrible time. He lost everything yet he refused to see it as God's doing – unlike everyone around him.

He clung to his belief in a good and just God and was sustained by it. Like the exposed bare trees in winter, there was something beautiful about his fierce faith.

He did not disappoint.

"The devil, like an adversary prowls around seeking someone to devour," Peter writes.

Sometimes strong faith seems to invite hard times, as if the devil wants to break God's people. I was reading in the Book of Acts the other day about the occasion when Paul freed a young girl with a spirit of divination. It must have been an incredible experience, proving once again the power of God, but the reward was that the men who were using her to make money dragged Paul and Silas before the magistrates where they were judged, severely flogged, thrown into prison and clapped in irons.

It was a very bleak situation, yet through it the beauty of their faith was exposed. What lay beneath the showiness of the miracles was praise and trust in God. They sat there in chains singing hymns, not knowing what would happen next. Deliverance came as they were miraculously freed and the jailer and his family were converted. With hindsight it was wonderful, but when he was in that dark, stripped-back situation, Paul had no idea when or if he would be freed, and how.

Similarly, when Paul is under house arrest in Rome, it appears as if his ministry is at an end. There can be no more travelling, no more planting churches or visiting established ones. You might say it's a winter experience.

Yet Paul uses it as an opportunity to witness to his captors, and he says that his imprisonment has turned out for good because the believers have been encouraged and strengthened by it. He goes on to say that he has learned to be content in all circumstances. He doesn't kick against the winter times. He's learned to trust God and to know that he is just a part of a wider plan. I see great beauty in Paul's acceptance of his reduced circumstances.

I have a friend who's suffered from a debilitating illness for many years. He and his wife recently retired and had plans for all the things they were going to do – travel, hobbies, church involvement. Unfortunately little of this has come to fruition because of health concerns. It seems like they've entered winter when they'd planned on it being spring and summer.

Yet my friend's attitude is to say that God is in control and it's his timing. Sometimes God needs to teach us stuff in the spiritual winter we experience from time to time. Nothing is ever wasted.

The other thing to remember is what the writer to the Hebrews states, that we are "surrounded by a great cloud of witnesses." Others have gone before us, they have been here and done it and now they watch the earthly church. I like to think they encourage us and cheer us on to glorify our God in all things.

We're not alone. We're on a team. And so we are not broken. No-one can break us in Christ. Even winter has its purpose. Tough times can be a time of beauty, too, as God hones us into something beautiful in the kingdom. ■

iStock.

Nature's Calendar For Winter

Thailand's Monkey Buffet Festival takes place in late November each year just outside Bangkok. Four thousand kgs of fruit, vegetables and other goodies are piled up for the benefit of the estimated 3,000 monkeys that live in the area.

In Alberta, Canada, Lake Abraham freezes and along with it the methane produced by bacteria living near the bottom. The gas gets trapped in perfect frozen bubbles. It's beautiful, but these pockets of gas are highly flammable.

iStock.

Brimstone butterflies in the UK, like some other species, produce a type of alcohol in their blood during winter that works as a natural anti-freeze. They're the UK's toughest butterflies, often spending the winter out amongst ivy or the leaves of evergreens.

Kale has seen a resurgence in popularity recently, and no wonder, as it reportedly contains more iron and calcium than any meat. Its name might come from the word "cawul", a Scottish and northern English word for cabbage.

Some varieties of heather, mainly cultivars of Erica carnea and Erica x darleyensis, continue to flower all year round. Kept in pots, they'll bring a welcome splash of colour in the darker months.

"No animal, according to the rules of animal etiquette, is ever expected to do anything strenuous, or heroic, or even moderately active during the off-season of winter."

– Kenneth Grahame

This Special Hour

SEE the twilight, deep and peaceful,
Stealing o'er the weary day,
While the passing sleepy cloudlets
Homeward drift upon their way.

See the grass in rhythmic swaying
Billow in the wind's caress,
While the whispering trees keep vigil
In their twilight evening dress.

See the drowsy flowers nodding,
Drifting gently to and fro
As the waves against the coral,
Timeless in their endless flow.

Soon these wonders of creation,
Country scene, and bird at nest,
Gather strength for morning's promise;
Nature at her season's best!

– Elizabeth Gozney.

Dragons

I'VE been out there fighting dragons,
I've been doing it all day.
First the dragons of Sheer Laziness,
Procrastination and Delay.

For when I switched on my computer,
To write a line or two
I went straight into my e-mails,
You know, the way you do.

Soon the dragon of Time Flying
Was breathing down my ear,
And from the ringing of my phone
The one of Idle Chat was near.

Now, facing dragons is a challenge,
And I knew I must be brave.
Recalling tales of old St George,
The day I had to save!

So determination triumphed,
I wrote this line or two.
Mine's a poem to remember
If those dragons bother you!

– Marian Cleworth.

The Pearl

FAR down below the surface
Of the deepest ocean sea
Is formed a natural miracle
Most wonderful to me.

Some say it is a nacre layer
That coats a grain of sand;
I say it is a miracle
I cannot understand.

Some say it's formed from crystalline
Deposited in tiers,
That lies within a mollusc clam
Which grows throughout the years.

Some say it is an object
Like a stone that lies within;
I say it is the heart's own pearl
Where life and love begin.

So when you think of treasure,
Think that, deep within the sea,
Lies a pearl imprisoned in a shell
Most people cannot see.

A highly valued precious jewel
Of beauty that is rare,
And then think of a heart's love –
That you might then compare.

– Dawn Lawrence.

Magic Land

FORESTS of pine trees and rivers that flow,
Where mountains soar high and doff caps of white snow,
Lochs stirred by the breeze and proud stags on the run,
Such is the place where nostalgia is spun.
Purple heather that blooms and curlews that call,
Salmon that leap and ne'er fail to enthrall.
Highlands and islands that dazzle the eye
Whilst eagles and kestrels hover and fly.
Famous names come to mind – Rob Roy, Burns and Lauder,
In this magic land that lies north of the border.

– Brian H. Gent.

Wings

BY word or deed I cannot tell
The joy that comes to me from flight;
The thought of leaning on the wind,
Fills me with a strange delight.
The distance that a bird can fly
Brings to my mind a wealth of things;
An arrow that swiftly cleaves the air
Gives to my spirit secret wings.

Flight also means the bird has flown
Beyond the rainbow and the snow;
Beyond the tears, the foolish fears,
To find a world I used to know:
There, as a bubble light, I float,
As fragile as a waking dream,
Then wake to feel the bubble break,
And think of that which might have been.

The air I breathe, the air I ride,
Bears me through a world of light,
I wonder if it seems as sweet
To swallows in their flight.
It calls to me – it sings to me,
That wind on wings of flame,
And where it leads my heart must go
To fly with it again.

– Dawn Lawrence.

Transforming Ted

NOW here's a thing, a mystery,
A puzzle, there's no doubt.
But maybe, all together,
We can work the answer out.

But first, go to a toy shop,
And buy a teddy bear,
Gift it to a little child ,
Then go and leave it there.

Yes, leave it there, do not return
For, oh, well, quite some time,
So it may dwell within a world
Of make-believe and rhyme.

Then, when at last you do return,
A wondrous change is there,
For something strange has happened
To that ordinary bear.

Transformed and quite transmuted,
No longer just an "it",
Now known by name, and what is more
A name which seems to fit.

Our furry friend may now have signs
Of wear and even tear.
It takes a lot of hugging
To show how much you care.

And so, back to my question . . .
However can it be
This bear of mass production
Now has PERSONALITY?

You may say I imagine it,
But when push comes to shove
My money's on the alchemy
Of sticky-fingered love.

– Tricia Sturgeon.

To A Daughter

THERE are so few words that can be said
To honestly address
A mother's feelings for a daughter
In a way she can express:

When I hear you speaking
Whether near or from afar,
Your voice lights up the darkest space
To take me where you are.

And when I'm in a room with you,
Somehow I always find
Your beauty and intelligence
Are of a special kind.

A kind that comes from gentleness;
Understanding; selflessness;
And all those loved ingredients
That only YOU possess.

It's said we each need joy in life
To carry each day through,
And that, I've found, is certainly
The gift I have, with you.

With you, I have a special friend,
And blessings in disguise;
It's no wonder that a daughter
Is considered such a prize!

– Dawn Lawrence.

from the Manse Window

A Very Important Place

A MAN woke up one morning to discover two birds flying around his home. Somehow they had managed to get in during the night!

He opened all the doors and windows, front and back, in the hope that they would find their escape, but to no avail. He tried to "shoo" them out but the poor birds just became even more panic-stricken, flapping about madly.

In his frustration the man saw they could not understand that he was trying to help them.

If I could just become one of them I could show them the way out, he thought.

If I could just become one of them . . .

"The word was made flesh and dwelt among us," we read in St John's gospel.

All throughout the Old Testament, God had been trying to tell his people how to free themselves – from doubt, from fear and from sin. But because they couldn't, God decided to show them . . . and to show us.

In the fullness of time the prophesies were fulfilled and God's anointed one had come into the world in the flesh. Immanuel had come to Israel, and it all happened at Bethlehem in Judea.

Bethlehem had certainly a long history. Uniquely it was the home of David the shepherd boy, who in time became Israel's king. Earlier still it was at Bethlehem, or certainly around Bethlehem, that Jacob had buried Rachel and had set up a stone beside her grave by which to remember her. Additionally it was there in Bethlehem that Ruth of the Old Testament had lived when she married Boaz.

In former days Bethlehem had certainly featured in the history of Israel, but essentially it was a small, quiet town, a village even, and by the time its name reappeared in the New Testament, it was really a quite unimportant village. In fact, it was a bit of a backwater and off the beaten track.

Indeed, 700 years before Jesus was born there, one of the many prophets, Micah, gave a graphic description of this "little town".

"But you Bethlehem, small as you are to be among Judah's

iStock.

By the Rev. Ian W.F. Hamilton.

clans, out of you shall come forth a governor for Israel."

So in God's good time the fulfilment of that prophesy made this little, unimportant village called Bethlehem most important indeed!

We then move to an unimportant venue. One would normally expect a king to be born into a beautiful palace or into some strong, secure castle. But not this king. The venue of his place of birth was a dark and draughty cave-stable attached to a roadside inn.

Joseph led his betrothed, Mary, and the donkey inside. They would just have to make the best of it; after all, it was only for one night.

But what a night it turned out to be! There, in this open stall in a crowded public inn, Jesus Christ was born and God became one of us.

Mary took her baby, we're told, and "wrapped him in swaddling clothes and laid him in a manger", which was in effect a small box out of which the cattle ate. That had to serve as the Saviour king's first cradle.

And so this unimportant, crude venue was the first resting-place of the Saviour of the world. But just think, if that cave-stable could be found today, how important it would be now, and how valuable. An importance, a value which came because Jesus came!

Mary of Nazareth was espoused to Joseph, the village carpenter, "espoused" meaning something similar to our word "engaged" but probably a bit more than that. The Jews considered the espousal to be a quite unbreakable relationship. It was almost as binding as marriage itself.

Mary was a simple Jewish country girl, and in her country the women folk worked very hard indeed, mainly in the fields and in their family homes. No doubt she assisted with the milking, the sewing, the baking, the fetching of water, the gathering of the firewood, the spinning of the wool, the weaving of the cloth and making garments for herself and her family . . . all the very mundane ordinary jobs. That's the kind of family we believe she belonged to, that's the kind of girl we believe she was, a typical ordinary village lass.

But an ordinary village lass who was highly favoured to be chosen by God for the most important and extraordinary responsibility, namely to be the mother of the world's Saviour. Mary knew well that it was every Jewish girl's wish to be the mother of God's Messiah, but when the angel had previously appeared and delivered the divine commission to her she was absolutely stunned to silence.

Maybe she had been taught in her earlier years that God's Messiah, God's king, would have had a queen for a mother, or certainly some woman of great importance or of high estate.

Mary was not an important person at all, and she realised this full well. She was betrothed to a village carpenter-cum-handyman. But once again the unimportant became very important, because God was involved.

The unimportant virgin became a very important person indeed because of the divine role she played in helping God to become one of us.

iStock.

A village, a venue, a virgin. Each of little importance, but all chosen by God to be a dwelling-place for Christ his son.

"If only I could become one of them," the man who was having trouble with his feathered friends who overnight had flown into his home thought.

At Bethlehem in Judea God did become one of them; he became one of us in order to show us the way out to freedom, to peace and to life in all its fullness.

That's what made the village, the venue and the virgin important . . . and that is who makes every one of us a very important person indeed.

Glory be to God on high! ■

Nature's Calendar For Winter

In flat deserts, thin ice layers that freeze at night then melt during the day can move rocks around at up to five metres per minute. The rocks are known as sailing stones. Rough-bottomed ones tend to travel straight, and smooth-bottomed ones tend to wander.

Beavers become hermits during the winter, staying inside their lodges and living off stored food and the reserves of fat in their tails. But with no cues as to when it's day or night, the beaver loses any sense of time and can often stay active for up to 29 hours at a time.

iStock

Help the hardy birds that have stayed with us – or are visiting us – for winter by putting up fat balls and seeds, as well as getting nest boxes up. National Nest Box Week takes place in February every year, to help birds who have lost a lot of natural nesting sites as gardens are increasingly less wild and old buildings are disappearing fast.

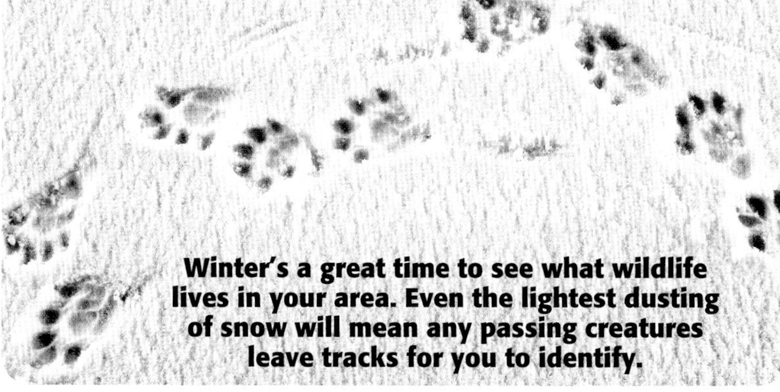

Winter's a great time to see what wildlife lives in your area. Even the lightest dusting of snow will mean any passing creatures leave tracks for you to identify.

Trim back petunias before the first frost and transfer them into pots. You can then bring them indoors for the winter, making sure there are no bugs on board!

"Isn't it true that a pleasant house makes winter more poetic, and doesn't winter add to the poetry of a house?"

– Charles Baudelaire

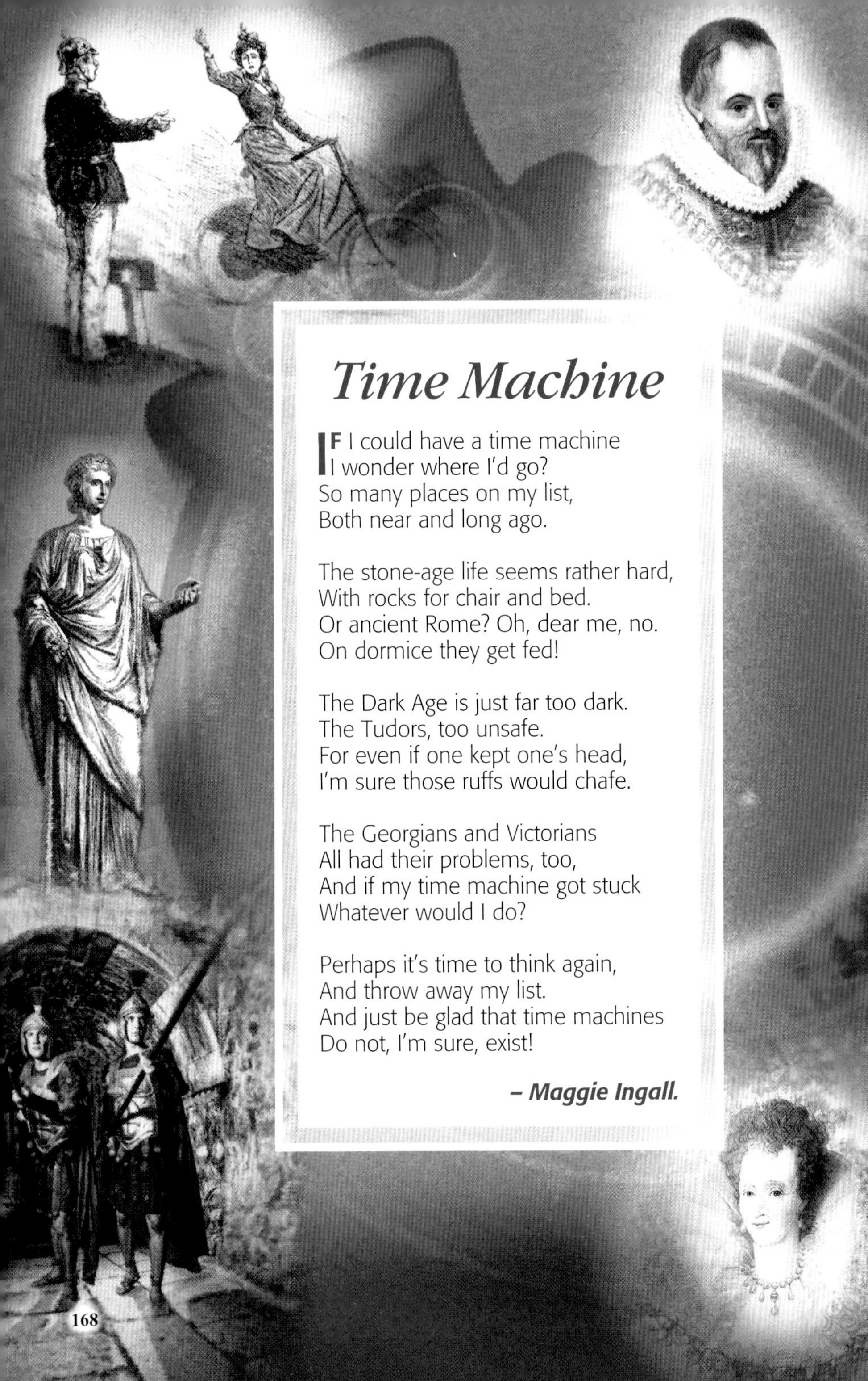

Time Machine

IF I could have a time machine
I wonder where I'd go?
So many places on my list,
Both near and long ago.

The stone-age life seems rather hard,
With rocks for chair and bed.
Or ancient Rome? Oh, dear me, no.
On dormice they get fed!

The Dark Age is just far too dark.
The Tudors, too unsafe.
For even if one kept one's head,
I'm sure those ruffs would chafe.

The Georgians and Victorians
All had their problems, too,
And if my time machine got stuck
Whatever would I do?

Perhaps it's time to think again,
And throw away my list.
And just be glad that time machines
Do not, I'm sure, exist!

– Maggie Ingall.

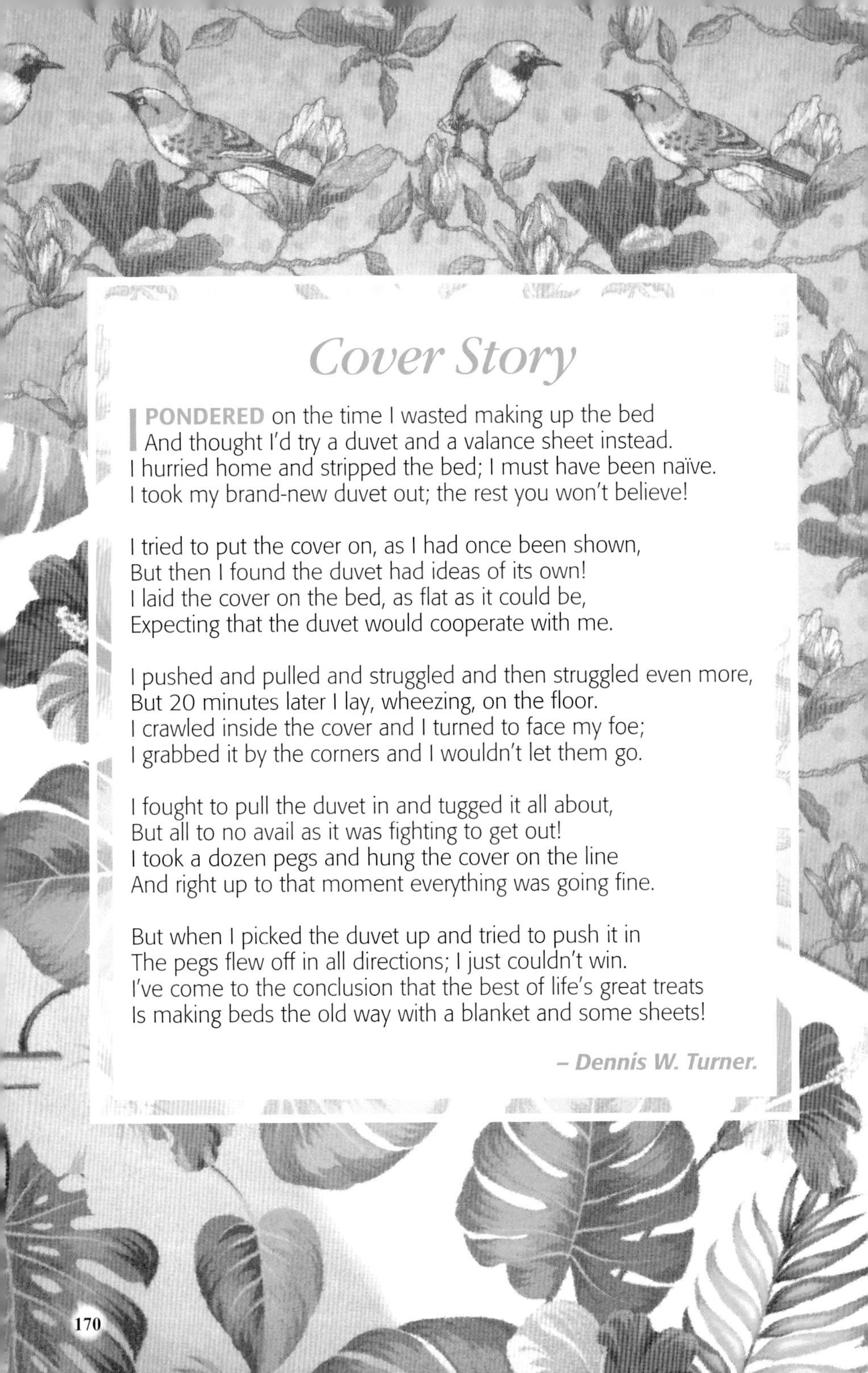

Cover Story

I PONDERED on the time I wasted making up the bed
And thought I'd try a duvet and a valance sheet instead.
I hurried home and stripped the bed; I must have been naïve.
I took my brand-new duvet out; the rest you won't believe!

I tried to put the cover on, as I had once been shown,
But then I found the duvet had ideas of its own!
I laid the cover on the bed, as flat as it could be,
Expecting that the duvet would cooperate with me.

I pushed and pulled and struggled and then struggled even more,
But 20 minutes later I lay, wheezing, on the floor.
I crawled inside the cover and I turned to face my foe;
I grabbed it by the corners and I wouldn't let them go.

I fought to pull the duvet in and tugged it all about,
But all to no avail as it was fighting to get out!
I took a dozen pegs and hung the cover on the line
And right up to that moment everything was going fine.

But when I picked the duvet up and tried to push it in
The pegs flew off in all directions; I just couldn't win.
I've come to the conclusion that the best of life's great treats
Is making beds the old way with a blanket and some sheets!

– Dennis W. Turner.

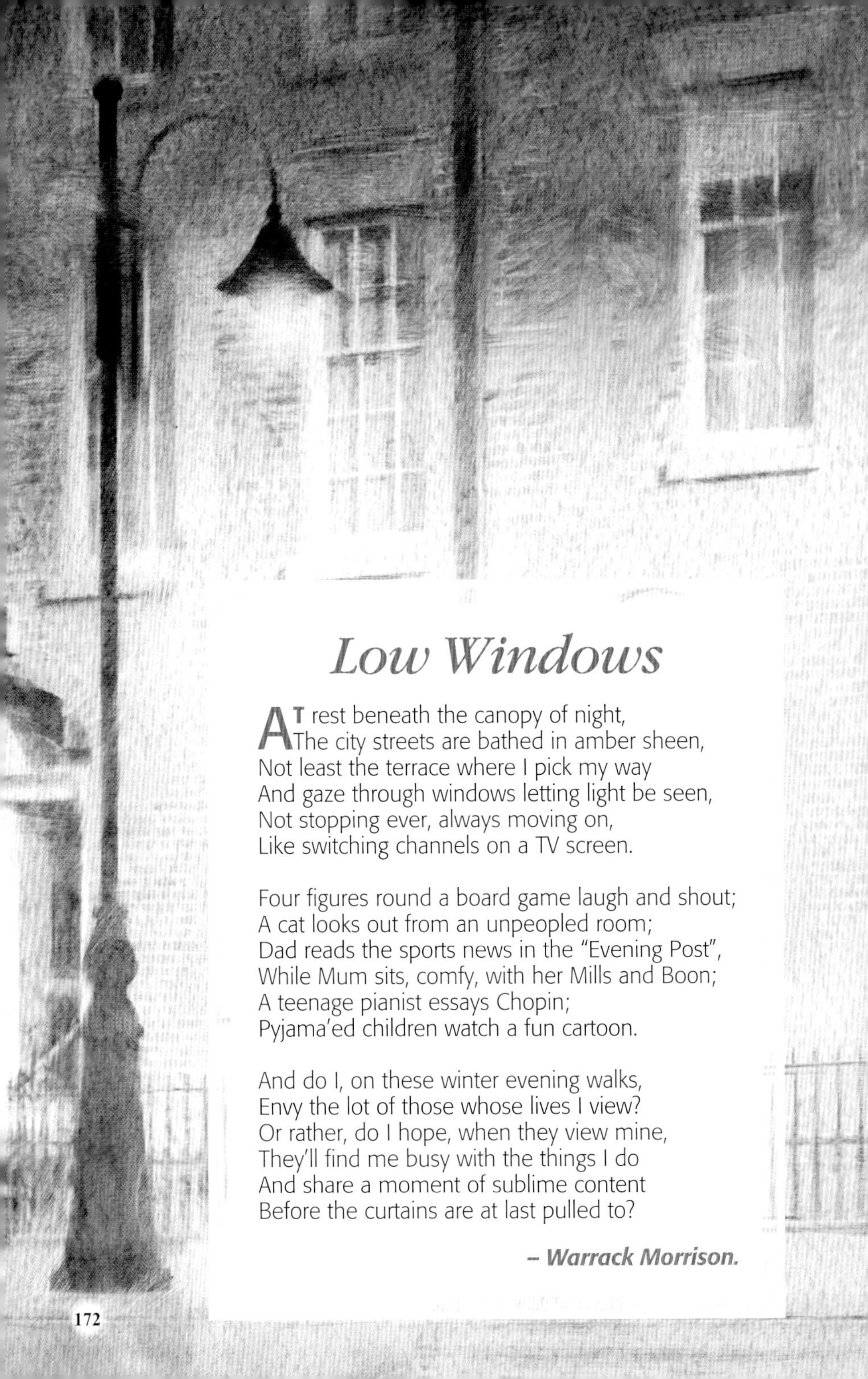

Low Windows

At rest beneath the canopy of night,
The city streets are bathed in amber sheen,
Not least the terrace where I pick my way
And gaze through windows letting light be seen,
Not stopping ever, always moving on,
Like switching channels on a TV screen.

Four figures round a board game laugh and shout;
A cat looks out from an unpeopled room;
Dad reads the sports news in the "Evening Post",
While Mum sits, comfy, with her Mills and Boon;
A teenage pianist essays Chopin;
Pyjama'ed children watch a fun cartoon.

And do I, on these winter evening walks,
Envy the lot of those whose lives I view?
Or rather, do I hope, when they view mine,
They'll find me busy with the things I do
And share a moment of sublime content
Before the curtains are at last pulled to?

– Warrack Morrison.

"A friend is a gift
you give yourself."
– Robert Louis Stevenson.